Table of Contents

STEVEN MANN

PowerShell™ for SharePoint® 2013

HOW-TO

SAMS | 800 East 96th Street, Indianapolis, Indiana 46240 USA

PowerShell™ for SharePoint® 2013 How-To

Copyright © 2013 by Pearson Education, Inc.

ISBN-13: 978-0-672-33691-1
ISBN-10: 0-672-33691-X

The Library of Congress cataloging-in-publication data is on file.

Printed in the United States of America

First Printing February 2013

Trademarks

All terms mentioned in this book that are known to be trademarks or service marks have been appropriately capitalized. Sams Publishing cannot attest to the accuracy of this information. Use of a term in this book should not be regarded as affecting the validity of any trademark or service mark.

Warning and Disclaimer

Every effort has been made to make this book as complete and as accurate as possible, but no warranty or fitness is implied. The information provided is on an "as is" basis. The author and the publisher shall have neither liability nor responsibility to any person or entity with respect to any loss or damages arising from the information contained in this book or from the use of programs accompanying it.

Bulk Sales

Sams Publishing offers excellent discounts on this book when ordered in quantity for bulk purchases or special sales. For more information, please contact

U.S. Corporate and Government Sales

1-800-382-3419

corpsales@pearsontechgroup.com

For sales outside of the U.S., please contact

International Sales

international@pearsoned.com

Editor-in-Chief
Greg Wiegand

Acquisitions Editor
Neil Rowe

Development Editor
Mark Renfrow

Managing Editor
Kristy Hart

Project Editor
Jovana Shirley

Copy Editor
Krista Hansing

Indexer
Lisa Stumpf

Proofreader
Kathy Ruiz

Technical Editor
J. Boyd Nolan

Editorial Assistant
Cindy Teeters

Cover Designer
Mark Shirar

Compositor
Nonie Ratcliff

About the Author

Steven Mann was born and raised in Philadelphia, Pennsylvania, where he still resides today. He is an Enterprise Applications Engineer for Morgan Lewis and has more than 19 years of professional experience.

Steven has authored and coauthored several books related to the subject of SharePoint Server, PowerShell, Managed Metadata, and Business Intelligence. Steven's blog site can be found at www.SteveTheManMann.com.

Acknowledgments

Thanks to Sams Publishing and Neil Rowe for making this book a reality and for giving me the opportunity to share my ideas and solutions.

We Want to Hear from You!

As the reader of this book, you are our most important critic and commentator. We value your opinion and want to know what we're doing right, what we could do better, what areas you'd like to see us publish in, and any other words of wisdom you're willing to pass our way.

We welcome your comments. You can email or write to let us know what you did or didn't like about this book—as well as what we can do to make our books better.

Please note that we cannot help you with technical problems related to the topic of this book.

When you write, please be sure to include this book's title and author as well as your name and email address. We will carefully review your comments and share them with the author and editors who worked on the book.

Email: consumer@samspublishing.com

Mail: Sams Publishing
 ATTN: Reader Feedback
 800 East 96th Street
 Indianapolis, IN 46240 USA

Reader Services

Visit our website and register this book at informit.com/register for convenient access to any updates, downloads, or errata that might be available for this book.

Introduction

Overview of This Book

PowerShell is becoming the de facto administration tool for Microsoft Server products. The capability to script reusable steps and code makes life easier for administrators, developers, and managers. With the latest release of Microsoft SharePoint Server 2013, PowerShell is the recommended administration tool. The previous stsadm console application is still available for backward compatibility, but it has been officially deprecated. Therefore, understanding the available cmdlets within SharePoint 2013 is essential.

This book is designed to provide a great reference of the SharePoint cmdlets across all areas and features within the product. The scenarios covered are helpful in building out both simple and complex scripts, using the syntax and examples in this book's chapters.

How to Benefit from This Book

This book provides a brief overview of how to get started with PowerShell in a SharePoint environment. It is not, however, a tutorial on PowerShell scripting itself. Use this book as a guide for performing repeated tasks or scripting steps that need to be replicated across your SharePoint environments (such as development, staging, and production).

Changes within the SharePoint 2013 cmdlets have taken place during various releases (for example, beta, release candidates, and product release). Many examples on the Internet use the old cmdlets and/or do not provide the appropriate parameters or types. In addition, some Internet documentation on the cmdlets, settings, and configurations is incorrect. You can rest assured that all the example command lines in this book have been tested and confirmed to be as accurate as possible.

You can access the code samples in this book by registering on the book's website at **informit.com/register**. Go to this URL, sign in, and enter the ISBN to register (free site registration required). After you register, look on your Account page, under Registered Products, for a link to Access Bonus Content.

How to Continue Expanding Your Knowledge

This book provides the basis for what is possible within PowerShell scripts for SharePoint. To become an overall PowerShell expert, you might want to expand your knowledge by exploring other books that discuss general PowerShell scripting techniques and syntax. Several general PowerShell books are available at informit.com.

CHAPTER 1

SharePoint 2013 Management Shell

IN THIS CHAPTER

- ▶ How Do I Run PowerShell?
- ▶ How Do I Make PowerShell Aware of SharePoint?
- ▶ What Is the SharePoint 2013 Management Shell?
- ▶ What Is the SharePoint 2013 Management Shell Loading?

This chapter is an overview of the PowerShell and SharePoint 2013 Management Shell console applications. It provides background information on the logistics behind running scripts for SharePoint.

How Do I Run PowerShell?

On every Windows Server running a variation of Windows Server 2008 or higher, PowerShell is installed and can be used for administration purposes. By default, the PowerShell application appears in the Windows taskbar. Right-clicking the application button displays available menu options, as shown in Figure 1.1.

FIGURE 1.1 The PowerShell application button provides a menu of options.

Selecting Import System Modules launches PowerShell and loads all modules from all services and server applications running on the current server. This is useful when scripting code for more than one set of services (such as SharePoint and SQL Server).

Selecting the Windows PowerShell ISE launches a pseudo-development environment in which you can create, execute, test, and debug PowerShell scripts. It is a glorified text editor but is helpful in creating and running scripts.

> **NOTE** Although PowerShell is automatically installed using Windows Server 2008 R2 and above, the ISE may or may not be activated depending on other server product installations. If it appears that the PowerShell ISE is not installed on the server, you must activate it as a server feature.

Selecting the Windows PowerShell menu item launches PowerShell in plain vanilla form (no additional modules or support for server applications—including SharePoint—are loaded). If you are not logged on as an administrator, select the Run As Administrator menu item to launch PowerShell with administrative privileges.

How Do I Make PowerShell Aware of SharePoint?

Launching PowerShell on the server opens a blue console application window. Without importing any modules, this instance does not know how to execute any SharePoint commands. To make this PowerShell instance aware of SharePoint, you must add the SharePoint PowerShell snap-in using the following command (as shown in Figure 1.2):

```
Add-PsSnapIn Microsoft.SharePoint.PowerShell
```

FIGURE 1.2 Adding the SharePoint PowerShell snap-in.

What Is the SharePoint 2013 Management Shell?

The SharePoint 2013 Management Shell is a variation of PowerShell geared toward the administration and management of SharePoint. After SharePoint is installed on the server, the management console is available from the Start menu, as shown in Figure 1.3.

Selecting the SharePoint 2013 Management Shell launches the management console, as shown in Figure 1.4.

The management console window knows about SharePoint commands, as well as general PowerShell commands, and is used to execute command lines or scripts. Chapter 2, "PowerShell Basics," describes the fundamental components of PowerShell.

FIGURE 1.3 SharePoint 2013 Management Shell on the Start menu.

FIGURE 1.4 SharePoint 2013 Management Shell console window.

What Is the SharePoint 2013 Management Shell Loading?

If you dig a little deeper and look at the properties of the SharePoint 2013 Management Shell menu item, you will notice that the SharePoint 2013 Management Shell involves nothing more than running PowerShell with a SharePoint script, as shown Figure 1.5.

The SharePoint script that the menu item is loading is located within the SharePoint 15 hive, under the PowerShell Registration folder, as shown in Figure 1.6.

FIGURE 1.5 SharePoint 2013 Management Shell properties.

FIGURE 1.6 SharePoint 2013 PowerShell Registration folder contents.

TIP Crack open some of the files located in the Registration folder to gain some insights on the SharePoint commands and operations.

CHAPTER 2

PowerShell Basics

This chapter explains some PowerShell basics, to help you acquire a general understanding. The sections and scenarios in this chapter help form a foundation for the tasks and solutions within this book.

What Is a Cmdlet?

PowerShell commands are called cmdlets. They are structured by a verb and noun concatenation in the form of verb-noun. So in the cmdlet Get-Help, Get is the verb and Help is the noun.

> **TIP** Use the Get-Help cmdlet to view helpful information about working with cmdlets.

How Can I See the Possible Verbs for a Noun Command?

If you know the noun but are unsure of the possible verbs available, you can enter the noun with -? to display the available verb-noun combinations. This also displays additional nouns that are similar to the one you provided. For example, SPSite -? displays the available verbs not only for the SPSite noun, but also for SPSiteAdministration, SPSiteSubscription, and other cmdlets available beginning with SPSite.

What Is a Parameter?

Most cmdlets need values to perform the desired actions. These values are provided to the cmdlet using parameters in the following form:

```
-parametername <value>
```

What Is a Switch Parameter?

A switch parameter is a parameter used with a cmdlet that does not take a value (or that is Boolean in nature and can be set to a false setting). The fact that the switch parameter is present "switches on" that option (true setting) when executing the cmdlet.

Most of the time, switch parameters are optional, but in some cases, you need to provide a switch. This depends on the cmdlet being executed.

How Can I See the Possible Parameters for a Cmdlet?

Entering the cmdlet in the console with -? as a parameter displays information about that cmdlet, along with the available parameters. Listing 2.1 shows an example.

LISTING 2.1. **Getting Information About a Cmdlet**

```
Get-SPSite -?
```

Some cmdlets, such as Get-SPSite, have different variations of parameters. These variations also are displayed within the information provided by the -? parameter, as Figure 2.1 shows.

FIGURE 2.1 Using -? with a cmdlet provides various syntax information.

What Does F3 Do?

Pressing the F3 function key in the console window displays the last-executed statement on the current prompt line. Using the up and down arrows, you can page through the other previous statements. This is useful for repeating or correcting previous command entries. Use the left and right arrow keys to place the cursor within the command text for corrections.

> **TIP** Pressing the Insert key on the keyboard allows you to overwrite text within the command text without pushing the text out.

What Does F7 Do?

This is probably the best-kept secret in command consoles. Every time I show this to someone, they say they had no idea it was available. If you have been entering several

commands in a console screen, pressing the F7 function key displays a menu of the previously executed commands, as Figure 2.2 shows.

FIGURE 2.2 Pressing the F7 function key presents a command history menu.

Use the arrow keys to change the selection in the menu. Pressing Enter executes the command selected. Pressing F9 on the menu enables you to enter the command number you want to re-execute but only places it on the line (the command is not executed automatically).

What Are Console Commands?

A handful of what I like to call console commands stem from the good ol' DOS days. They have been available in command prompts since then, with the current PowerShell consoles included. These commands provide standard directory navigation, file handling, and screen handling.

Several common console commands follow:

- ► cd: Changes the directory
- ► cls: Clears the console screen
- ► dir: Displays a listing of the current directory (folder)
- ► type: Used with a text-based filename and displays the contents of a text file

TIP These commands have been grouped within PowerShell as Aliases. To see all of the available aliases use Get-Alias.

Path Environment Variable

Scenario/Problem: You have scripts within a local folder which you want PowerShell to recognize such that you do not need to use the full path name.

Solution: Add the local directory path to the PSModulePath variable.

You add the local folder's path to the PSModule environment variable by entering the following command in the PowerShell command prompt (substituting `<folder path>` with the local directory path), as shown in Listing 2.2.

LISTING 2.2 **Adding a Folder Path to the PSModulePath**

```
$env:PSModulePath = $env:PSModulePath + ";c:\<folder path>"
```

> **TIP** Add the same exact command line into the PowerShell profile configuration file to always have your local folder added to the PSModulePath. See http://technet. microsoft.com/en-us/library/dd315342.aspx for more information about PowerShell profiles.

Running Unsigned Scripts

Scenario/Problem: You need to be able to run unsigned scripts within PowerShell.

Solution: Use the Set-ExecutionPolicy command.

To run unsigned scripts, you must change the execution policy:

```
Set-ExecutionPolicy remotesigned
```

You are prompted with a confirmation. Enter Y and press Enter (or just press Enter—Y is the default).

In some cases, you must set the policy to Unrestricted:

```
Set-ExecutionPolicy unrestricted
```

> **TIP** For more information on signing scripts, see http://technet.microsoft.com/ en-us/library/dd347649.aspx

Disabling the Confirmation Prompt

Scenario/Problem: You need to automatically confirm operations such that a script runs unattended.

Solution: Include the -`Confirm` parameter with a `$false` setting.

When running cmdlets discussed in this book, you might receive a confirmation message to confirm the action being processed. If you use these cmdlets in scripts, the script will not run straight through without prompting for the confirmation.

The cmdlets that have a -`Confirm` optional parameter can be called in unattended mode by passing in -`Confirm:$false` to the cmdlet, as shown in Listing 2.3.

LISTING 2.3 **Suppressing the Confirmation Prompt Example**

```
Remove-item *.png -Confirm:$false
```

NOTE Not all cmdlets have a -`Confirm` parameter. Use the help (`-?`) parameter to verify each cmdlet in question.

Generating Inline Credentials

Scenario/Problem: You need to provide cmdlets with credentials without prompting for them.

Solution: Create a new `PSCredential` object.

Various cmdlets discussed in this book require SharePoint and/or SQL Server account credentials for proper authentication when performing the desired operations. The examples include using (`Get-Credential`) as the parameter value, which prompts the user for credentials.

When running these cmdlets in scripts, the prompting for credentials pauses the execution. If you need the script to run straight through, instead of using `Get-Credential`, you can generate a new `PSCredential` object inline, as shown in Listing 2.4.

LISTING 2.4 **Generating Inline Credentials Example**

```
(New-Object System.Management.Automation.PSCredential "domain\user",
(ConvertTo-SecureString "password" -AsPlainText -Force))
```

Therefore, simply substitute (Get-Credential) for the text shown in Listing 2.4 with the proper username and password when using a cmdlet with authentication requirements.

Referencing an Assembly

Scenario/Problem: You want to be able to call methods and/or use objects within a trusted assembly (DLL).

Solution: Use a reflection declaration, and then use a variable to instantiate an object.

You can reference an assembly in your PowerShell script and then use any objects available by assigning them to a variable. Then you can use any methods or properties within your script. No intellisense exists, so you need to know the object model beforehand. Listing 2.5 demonstrates an example assembly reference and usage.

LISTING 2.5 **Referencing and Using a SharePoint Assembly**

```
[Void][System.Reflection.Assembly]::LoadWithPartialName("Microsoft.
SharePoint")

[Void][System.Reflection.Assembly]::LoadWithPartialName("Microsoft.
SharePoint.Administration")

$spFarm = [Microsoft.SharePoint.Administration.SPFarm]::Local
$spFarmSolutions = $spFarm.Solutions
```

TIP Instead of coding and compiling a console application, use a PowerShell script that references the SharePoint assemblies.

CHAPTER 3

SharePoint Installation and Configuration

This chapter explores how to use PowerShell scripts to perform the installation and configuration of SharePoint 2013. Microsoft provides a set of tools that aids in the installation. Use these procedures to script and run unattended installations.

Prepare the Microsoft SharePoint Installation Module

Scenario/Problem: You need to have access to extended SharePoint installation commands within PowerShell.

Solution: Download and install the SPModule from Microsoft.

Before you can install SharePoint from within PowerShell, you need to download and install the SPModule code from Microsoft. The downloadable file is located at www.microsoft.com/downloads/en/details.aspx?FamilyID=c57556ff-8df0-44fd-aba6-3df01b9f80ce (or search for "SPModule PowerShell").

Unzip the file and place it into a local folder. Add this folder to the PSModulePath environment variable. The code is unsigned, so you must allow unsigned scripts to run. See Chapter 2, "PowerShell Basics," for steps on adding an environment variable and allowing the execution of unsigned scripts.

Launch Windows PowerShell by right-clicking the icon and selecting Run As Administrator. Import the modules extracted from the zipped SPModule by using the commands in Listing 3.1.

LISTING 3.1 **Importing the SPModule Components**

```
Import-Module SPModule.misc
Import-Module SPModule.setup
```

TIP You must set your execution policy to Unrestricted to successfully import the SPModule.misc and SPModule.setup files. You therefore are prompted upon import of some scripts. Entering an **R** for Run Once installs the scripts properly.

The cmdlets to install and configure SharePoint are now installed and ready for use.

NOTE Importing the SPModule.misc file performs a check for updates. If updates are available, you are notified. Perform any updates before proceeding.

Install SharePoint Unattended

Scenario/Problem: You need to install SharePoint from PowerShell.

Solution: Use the `Install-SharePoint` cmdlet from the `SPModule`.

The first step in unattended installation and configuration is to install SharePoint onto the server. The `SPModule` provides the `Install-SharePoint` cmdlet to perform the installation. This cmdlet is used in conjunction with a setup configuration file that contains the installation parameters.

The SharePoint installation disc includes sample setup configuration files, located in their own folder within `Files`, as shown in Figure 3.1. Listing 3.2 shows an example of the configuration file contents.

FIGURE 3.1 Sample configuration files are contained within the folders shown.

LISTING 3.2 **Sample Farm Setup Configuration File**

```
<Configuration>
    <Package Id="sts">
        <Setting Id="LAUNCHEDFROMSETUPSTS" Value="Yes"/>
    </Package>

    <Package Id="spswfe">
        <Setting Id="SETUPCALLED" Value="1"/>
    </Package>
```

```
    <Logging Type="verbose" Path="%temp%"
Template="SharePoint Server Setup(*).log"/>
    <!--<PIDKEY Value="Enter Product Key Here" />-->
    <Setting Id="SERVERROLE" Value="APPLICATION"/>
    <Setting Id="USINGUIINSTALLMODE" Value="1"/>
    <Setting Id="SETUPTYPE" Value="CLEAN_INSTALL"/>
    <Setting Id="SETUP_REBOOT" Value="Never"/>
</Configuration>
```

Copy the `config.xml` file that matches your intended installation to a local drive location. Open the file in Notepad and uncomment the `PIDKEY` line by removing the `<!--` from the front and the `-->` from the back. Enter your SharePoint product key in place of `Enter Product Key Here`. Save your changes.

You can now use this configuration file with the `Import-SharePoint` cmdlet, which has the following syntax:

```
Install-SharePoint -setupexepath <path to setup.exe on disc>
-configxmlpath <path to the setup config.xml>
```

Listing 3.3 shows a sample command-line entry.

LISTING 3.3 **Installing SharePoint from the Command Line**

```
Install-SharePoint -setupexepath D:\setup.exe -configxmlpath
c:\config.xml
```

SharePoint is installed on the server accordingly.

> **TIP** Install SharePoint on all servers that will participate in the farm (except for the database server) before configuring a new farm or joining an existing farm.

Install Without a Product Key in the Configuration File

For security purposes, you might not want to store the product key within the configuration file. Instead, you can use the `-PIDKey` parameter, followed by your product key in quotes on the command line with the `Install-SharePoint` cmdlet, as in Listing 3.4.

LISTING 3.4 **Installing SharePoint from the Command Line with a Product Key**

```
Install-SharePoint -setupexepath D:\setup.exe -configxmlpath
c:\config.xml -PIDKey "ABDCE-FGHIJ-KLMNO-PQRST-UVWXY"
```

Configure a New SharePoint Farm

Scenario/Problem: You need to configure a new SharePoint farm from the command line.

Solution: Use the `New-SharePointFarm` cmdlet from the `SPModule`.

The `New-SharePointFarm` cmdlet enables you to configure a new SharePoint farm on the server. The syntax follows:

```
New-SharePointFarm -databaseserver <server name>
-databaseaccessaccount (Get-Credential <domain\account>)
-farmname <name of new farm>
-passphrase (ConvertTo-SecureString -asplaintext -force -string "Enter a
farm pass phrase here")
```

This command requires credentials for the database server. Therefore, the `Get-Credential` PowerShell command is used in conjunction with `New-SharePointFarm`. After you enter the command, PowerShell prompts you for the password of the database access account entered, as in Figure 3.2.

> **TIP** Use inline credentials instead of (`Get-Credential`). See Chapter 2 for more details.

FIGURE 3.2 Using `Get-Credential` prompts for the corresponding password.

After you enter the credentials, the new farm is configured using the database server entered. This essentially creates the `SharePoint_Config` database and prepares the farm for use.

> **NOTE** The farm passphrase is a password that is used when you are adding new servers to the farm or making farm configuration changes. It needs to be entered into the cmdlet as a secure string; therefore, the `ConvertTo-SecureString` cmdlet is also used in conjunction with `New_SharePointFarm`.

Join a Server to the SharePoint Farm

Scenario/Problem: You need to join the servers to the new SharePoint farm.

Solution: Use the `Join-SharePointFarm` cmdlet from the `SPModule`.

The previous cmdlet (`New-SharePointFarm`) created the database and configured the SharePoint farm. You cannot run this again on the other servers. Instead, you need to join the servers to the farm using the `Join-SharePointFarm` cmdlet:

```
Join-SharePointFarm -databaseserver <database server name>
-configurationdatabasename <config database>
-passphrase (ConvertTo-SecureString -asplaintext -force -string
"<farm pass phrase>")
```

The farm passphrase used with the `Join-SharePointFarm` cmdlet should be the same passphrase used when you are creating the new SharePoint farm.

Create a New Web Application

Scenario/Problem: You need to create a new web application for the SharePoint farm.

Solution: Use the `New-SPWebApplication` cmdlet from the SharePoint 2013 Management Shell.

You can now use the SharePoint 2013 Management Shell because SharePoint has been installed and the `SPModule` commands have been utilized. If you are running a full script and/or still want to use the PowerShell console, be sure to add the `SharePoint` snap-in (`Add-PsSnapin Microsoft.SharePoint.PowerShell`) so that the SharePoint cmdlets are available.

To add a new web application, use the New-SPWebApplication cmdlet as follows:

```
New-SPWebApplication -applicationpool <name of new application pool>
-name <name of new web app>
-applicationpoolaccount <service account to be used for the
application pool> -port <desired port number>
```

Listing 3.5 shows a sample command-line entry for creating the main SharePoint web application.

LISTING 3.5 **Creating a New Web Application**

```
New-SPWebApplication -applicationpool SharePoint-80
-name SharePoint-80 -applicationpoolaccount SP\AppPoolAccount -port 80
```

This process might take a few minutes. When it completes, the console presents the display name and the URL of the new web application.

> **TIP** If you do not include the port number, a random port number will be assigned. The first web application created will use port 80.

Create a New Site Collection

> **Scenario/Problem:** You need to create a new top-level site collection.

Solution: Use the New-SPSite cmdlet from the SharePoint 2013 Management Shell.

To add a new site collection, use the New-SPSite cmdlet as follows:

```
New-SPSite -url <full url of new site collection>
-name <name of new site collection>
-owneralias <site collection administrator>
-template <site collection template to use>
```

Listing 3.6 shows a sample command-line entry for creating the root site collection using the Team Site template.

LISTING 3.6 **Creating the Root Top-Level Site Collection**

```
New-SPSite -url http://sp2013/ -name Home -owneralias SP\SiteAdmin
-template STS#0
```

You can find the site template names using `Get-SPWebTemplate`. If no template is provided, the site collection is still created. In this case, after the site is accessed via the browser, SharePoint prompts for the selection of a site collection template.

Create a New Subsite

Scenario/Problem: You want to create sites under your site collection.

Solution: Use the `New-SPWeb` cmdlet from the SharePoint 2013 Management Shell.

To add a new subsite, use the `New-SPWeb` cmdlet as follows:

```
New-SPWeb -url <full url of new site> -name <name of new site>
-template <site template to use>
```

A few switch parameters are available for the `New-SPWeb` cmdlet:

- ▶ `AddToTopNav`
- ▶ `UniquePermissions`
- ▶ `UseParentTopNav`

The `AddToTopNav` switch parameter places the new site within the top navigation of the site collection. Using the `UseParentTopNav` switch parameter replicates the top nav of the site collection onto the new subsite. Creating a site with `UniquePermissions` forces the site to not inherit permissions from the site collection and only grants the System Account Full Control access.

Listing 3.7 shows a sample command-line entry for creating a subsite using the Team Site template.

LISTING 3.7 **Creating a Subsite in the Root Site Collection**

```
New-SPWeb -url http://sp2013/PSSubSite -name "PS Sub Site"
-template STS#0 -AddToTopNav -UniquePermissions -UseParentTopNav
```

You can find the site template names using `Get-SPWebTemplate`. If no template is provided, the site still is created. In this case, after the site is accessed via the browser, SharePoint prompts for the selection of a site template.

Using both `AddToTopNav` and `UseParentTopNav` ensures that the new site always appears in the top navigation, as shown in Figure 3.3.

FIGURE 3.3 Using the switch parameters places the subsite in the top nav.

CHAPTER 4

Farm Management

This chapter outlines the SharePoint PowerShell commands that manage general operations within your SharePoint farm. Whereas some operations are specific to the farm level, others are overall farm administration cmdlets that cannot be categorized into a separate chapter.

Review Farm Configuration Values

Scenario/Problem: You want to see the farm configuration values.

Solution: Use the `Get-SPFarmConfig` cmdlet without any parameters.

Several configuration settings are available using `SPFarmConfig`. Execute the `Get-SPFarmConfig` without any parameters, as shown in Listing 4.1, to display the current values. Figure 4.1 shows some sample output.

LISTING 4.1 **Displaying All Farm Configuration Values**

```
Get-SPFarmConfig
```

FIGURE 4.1 `Get-SPFarmConfig` displays the current farm values.

This is not the most exciting list of configuration values; however, they could impact the behavior of your SharePoint farm. The next section explains how to change these values.

Set the Farm Configuration Values

Scenario/Problem: You want to modify the farm configuration values displayed in the previous section.

Solution: Use the `Set-SPFarmConfig` cmdlet with the configuration parameters.

You can modify the values in the previous section using the `Set-SPFarmConfig` cmdlet with the associated parameter of each value. The parameters for these configuration values are as follows:

- `ASPScriptOptimizationEnabled`
- `DataFormWebPartAutoRefreshEnabled`
- `WorkflowBatchSize`
- `WorkflowEventDeliveryTimeout`
- `WorkflowPostponeThreshold`

The `ASPScriptOptimizationEnabled` parameter is a Boolean parameter that determines whether ASP scripting is allowed to be optimized by IIS.

The `DataFormWebPartAutoRefreshEnabled` parameter is a Boolean parameter that determines whether the data form web parts on the SharePoint web pages are allowed to automatically refresh using the asynchronous Ajax settings. If this value is set to `false`, the data form web parts will not automatically refresh, regardless of the web part Ajax settings.

The `WorkflowBatchSize` value defaults to `100` and determines the number of events that can be processed for a single workflow instance. The value must be greater than `0` but can be as large as the maximum integer value.

The `WorkflowEventDeliveryTimeout` parameter specifies the number of minutes that a workflow can run before it times out. The default value is `5` minutes, but it can be any positive integer. If the workflow times out, it is placed back into the queue to attempt execution again.

The `WorkflowPostponeThreshold` parameter determines how many workflows can operate at the same time. The default is `15` workflows, but this can be any integer value. If the number of workflows that need to run exceeds this amount, the excess workflows are placed in the queue and must wait for the running workflows to finish.

If you haven't noticed, the parameter names are exactly the same as in the output from `Get-SPFarmConfig`. Listing 4.2 shows a sample command line for setting these values.

LISTING 4.2 **Setting the Farm Configuration Values**

```
Set-SPFarmConfig -ASPScriptOptimizationEnabled:$true
-DataFormWebPartAutoRefreshEnabled:$false -WorkflowBatchSize 50
-WorkflowEventDeliveryTimeout 20 -WorkflowPostponeThreshold 10
```

Run the `Get-SPFarmConfig` cmdlet to verify your changes.

NOTE The `ASPScriptOptimizationEnabled` parameter is not documented as part of the cmdlet help but is indeed an accepted Boolean parameter for `Set—SPFarmConfig`.

Refresh Installed Products

Scenario/Problem: You need to ensure that the SharePoint products installed on a farm server are properly registered.

Solution: Use the `Set-SPFarmConfig` cmdlet with the `InstalledProductsRefresh` switch parameter.

Using the `InstalledProductsRefresh` switch parameter with the `Set-SPFarmConfig` cmdlet refreshes the current server's license state with the products installed on the SharePoint farm. Listing 4.3 shows a sample command line.

LISTING 4.3 **Refreshing the Installed Products**

```
Set-SPFarmConfig -InstalledProductsRefresh
```

Change the Port of Central Admin

Scenario/Problem: You want to change the HTTP port value for Central Administration.

Solution: Use the `Set-SPCentralAdministration` cmdlet with the `Port` parameter.

The `Set-SPCentralAdministration` cmdlet is used solely to change the port number configured for the Central Administration web application. Provide a valid port number, as shown in Listing 4.4.

LISTING 4.4 **Changing the Port of Central Admin**

```
Set-SPCentralAdministration -Port 20222
```

Change the Farm Passphrase

Scenario/Problem: You want to change the farm passphrase.

Solution: Use the `Set-SPPassPhrase` cmdlet with the `PassPhrase` parameter.

The Set-SPPassPhrase cmdlet is used solely to change the SharePoint farm pass-phrase. This passphrase was initially entered during the installation of the SharePoint farm. Provide a secure string value with the PassPhrase parameter, as shown in Listing 4.5.

LISTING 4.5 **Changing the Farm Passphrase**

```
Set-SPPassPhrase -PassPhrase (ConvertTo-SecureString -asplaintext
-force -string "SharePoint1")
```

For scripting purposes, if you do not want to be prompted to confirm the passphrase entry, include the ConfirmPassPhrase parameter and switch off the general confirma-tion, as shown in Listing 4.6.

LISTING 4.6 **Changing the Farm Passphrase Without Prompts**

```
Set-SPPassPhrase -PassPhrase (ConvertTo-SecureString -asplaintext
-force -string "SharePoint1") -ConfirmPassPhrase
(ConvertTo-SecureString -asplaintext -force -string "SharePoint1")
-Confirm:$false
```

> **TIP** The default operation performs the passphrase modification for the entire farm. If you run into issues, use the LocalServerOnly switch parameter to perform the modification on only the current server. Continue on each server in the farm to pinpoint the problem.

Retrieve the System Accounts

> **Scenario/Problem:** You need to retrieve system account objects.

Solution: Use the Get-SPProcessAccount cmdlet.

Issuing the Get-SPProcessAccount cmdlet without any parameters displays all system and managed accounts on the SharePoint farm, as shown in Figure 4.2.

Several mutually exclusive switch parameters can retrieve a specific system account. The switch parameters are LocalSystem, LocalService, and NetworkService. Use these separately, as shown in Listing 4.7.

LISTING 4.7 **Retrieving Individual System Accounts**

```
Get-SPProcessAccount -LocalSystem
Get-SPProcessAccount -LocalService
Get-SPProcessAccount -NetworkService
```

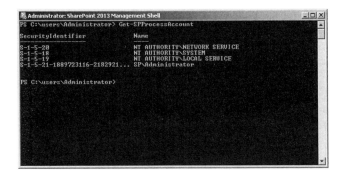

FIGURE 4.2 `Get-SPProcessAccount` displays all system and managed accounts.

> **TIP** Pipe the result to other cmdlets that accept process accounts or assign the result to a variable for use within a cmdlet script.

Retrieve Managed Accounts

> **Scenario/Problem:** You need to retrieve managed accounts on the farm.

Solution: Use the `Get-SPManagedAccount` cmdlet.

Issuing the `Get-SPManagedAccount` cmdlet without any parameters displays all managed accounts on the SharePoint farm. To retrieve a specific managed account, you can use the account name, as shown in Listing 4.8.

LISTING 4.8 **Retrieving a Specific Managed Account**

```
Get-SPManagedAccount "SP\Administrator"
```

> **TIP** Pipe the result to other cmdlets that accept managed accounts or assign the result to a variable for use within a cmdlet script.

Rename a Server on the Farm

> **Scenario/Problem:** You want to rename a server that participates in the SharePoint farm.

Solution: Use the `Rename-SPServer` cmdlet.

The Rename-SPServer cmdlet renames a server in the farm. However, note that it renames the server only from a SharePoint standpoint and does not actually rename the physical server. Use the current name as the Identity parameter and the new name for the Name parameter, as shown in Listing 4.9.

LISTING 4.9 **Renaming a Server on the Farm**

```
Rename-SPServer -Identity "OldServerName" -Name "NewServerName"
```

> **WARNING** If the rename procedure does not complete successfully, the server being renamed may no longer function as a SharePoint server. Running the SharePoint 2013 Products Configuration Wizard may resolve any issues; however, there is the potential of configuration database corruption forcing you to rebuild the SharePoint farm.

Display the Configured Managed Paths

> **Scenario/Problem:** You need to display the current managed paths configured on a web application in the farm.

Solution: Use the Get-SPManagedPath cmdlet with an associated web application.

Issuing the Get-SPManagedPath cmdlet with the WebApplication parameter (as shown in Listing 4.10) displays all configured managed paths on the SharePoint farm, as shown in Figure 4.3.

LISTING 4.10 **Retrieving Configured Managed Paths**

```
Get-SPManagedPath -WebApplication "SharePoint - 80"
```

FIGURE 4.3 Get-SPManagedPath displays all configured managed paths.

Create a New Managed Path

Scenario/Problem: You want to create a new managed path in a web application on the SharePoint farm.

Solution: Use the `New-SPManagedPath` cmdlet.

Using the `New-SPManagedPath` cmdlet enables you to create a new managed path on the specified web application, as shown in Listing 4.11.

LISTING 4.11 **Creating a New Managed Path**

```
New-SPManagedPath -WebApplication "SharePoint - 80"
-RelativeURL "/teamsites/"
```

The forward slashes (/) in the name of the managed path are optional but provide a visual queue (similar to manually creating a managed path through Central Administration).

By default, the managed path is created as a wildcard inclusion type. You can use the `Explicit` switch parameter to generate the managed path as an explicit inclusion type, as shown in Listing 4.12.

LISTING 4.12 **Creating a New Managed Path with Explicit Inclusion**

```
New-SPManagedPath -WebApplication "SharePoint - 80" -RelativeURL
"/departments/" -Explicit
```

TIP You may also create a managed path using the `HostHeader` parameter instead of the `WebApplication` parameter. `New-SPManagedPath` has two parameter sets for this purpose.

Remove a Managed Path

Scenario/Problem: You need to delete a managed path from a specific web application on your SharePoint farm.

Solution: Use the `Remove-SPManagedPath` cmdlet.

Using the `Remove-SPManagedPath` cmdlet enables you to remove a managed path from the specified web application, as shown in Listing 4.13.

LISTING 4.13 **Removing a Managed Path**

```
Remove-SPManagedPath -Identity "departments"
-WebApplication "SharePoint - 80"
```

> **TIP** You may also remove a managed path using the HostHeader parameter instead of the WebApplication parameter. Remove-SPManagedPath has two parameter sets for this purpose.

The Identity parameter is simply the name of the relative URL used to generate the managed path, which becomes the name of the managed path. Use the Get-SPManagedPath cmdlet to review the names.

Merge Log Files

> **Scenario/Problem:** You need to trace an issue but don't want to have to review the logs on each server in the farm.

Solution: Use the Merge-SPLogFile cmdlet.

The Merge-SPLogFile cmdlet is a wonderful process that consolidates the logs from all servers in the farm into one log file. This makes tracing and finding issues easier. Listing 4.14 shows a sample command line.

LISTING 4.14 **Merging Log Files**

```
Merge-SPLogFile -Path E:\Logs\MergedLog.log -StartTime "1/19/2013"
-Overwrite
```

The Path parameter is the path and filename of the log file you want to create. If it already exists, the cmdlet will fail unless you include the Overwrite switch parameter. You should use the StartTime parameter (and/or the EndTime parameter) to specify the range of the log entries to gather and merge.

Several other parameters can help you narrow the log search:

- Area
- Category
- ContextFilter
- Correlation
- Level

- EventID
- Message
- Process
- ThreadID

End the Current Log File

Scenario/Problem: You want SharePoint to be finished with the current log file and start a new one.

Solution: Use the `New-SPLogFile` cmdlet.

The `New-SPLogFile` cmdlet stops the current log file and starts a new one. This is helpful if you are tracing an issue and do not need more entries in the log file or do not want any issues with the log file being in use. Simply issue the `New-SPLogFile` cmdlet without any parameters on the server where you want to start a new log file, as shown in Listing 4.15.

LISTING 4.15 **Start a New Log File**

```
New-SPLogFile
```

Review SharePoint Designer Settings

Scenario/Problem: You need to review the overall SharePoint Designer settings for a particular web application on the SharePoint farm.

Solution: Use the `Get-SPDesignerSettings` cmdlet.

The `Get-SPDesignerSettings` cmdlet enables you to review the current SharePoint Designer settings for a specified web application. Running this cmdlet with the `WebApplication` parameter, shown in Listing 4.16, displays the current settings, as shown in Figure 4.4.

LISTING 4.16 **Reviewing the SharePoint Designer Settings**

```
Get-SPDesignerSettings -WebApplication "SharePoint - 80"
```

FIGURE 4.4 `Get-SPDesignerSettings` displays the SharePoint Designer settings.

Configure SharePoint Designer Settings

Scenario/Problem: You need to modify the overall SharePoint Designer settings for a particular web application on the SharePoint farm.

Solution: Use the `Set-SPDesignerSettings` cmdlet.

The `Set-SPDesignerSettings` cmdlet enables you to modify the SharePoint Designer settings for a specific web application. Each setting, listed here, is a Boolean parameter:

- `AllowDesigner`
- `AllowMasterPageEditing`
- `AllowRevertFromTemplate`
- `ShowURLStructure`

Listing 4.17 shows a sample modification command line.

LISTING 4.17 **Modifying the SharePoint Designer Settings**

```
Set-SPDesignerSettings -WebApplication "SharePoint - 80"
-AllowDesigner:$true -AllowMasterPageEditing:$false
-AllowRevertFromTemplate:$false -ShowURLStructure:$true
```

The `AllowDesigner` parameter determines whether the sites in the web application can be modified with SharePoint Designer. The user performing the action must have the proper permissions to modify the site. The default value is `True`.

The `AllowMasterPageEditing` parameter determines whether the master pages and page layouts in the sites of the web application can be modified with SharePoint Designer by site administrators or users with the appropriate permissions. The default value is `True`.

The `AllowRevertFromTemplate` parameter specifies whether site pages can be detached from the site definition using SharePoint Designer. The default value is `True`.

The `ShowURLStructure` parameter specifies whether the URL structure of the web application can be modified in SharePoint Designer. The default value is `True`.

> **TIP** Use `Get-SPDesignerSettings` to validate the modifications.

Review Workflow Configuration Settings

> **Scenario/Problem:** You need to review the overall workflow configuration settings for a particular web application on the SharePoint farm or a site collection.

Solution: Use the `Get-SPWorkflowConfig` cmdlet.

The `Get-SPWorkflowConfig` cmdlet enables you to review the current workflow configuration settings for a specified web application or site collection. Listing 4.18 illustrates running this cmdlet with the `WebApplication` parameter. Listing 4.19 shows the site collection command line. Figure 4.5 shows sample results of both command lines.

LISTING 4.18 **Reviewing the Workflow Configuration for a Web Application**

```
Get-SPWorkflowConfig -WebApplication "SharePoint - 80"
```

LISTING 4.19 **Reviewing the Workflow Configuration for a Site Collection**

```
Get-SPWorkflowConfig -SiteCollection "http://sp2013"
```

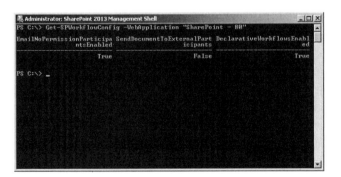

FIGURE 4.5 `Get-SPWorkflowConfig` displays the workflow configuration settings.

Modify Workflow Configuration Settings

Scenario/Problem: You need to modify the overall SharePoint Designer settings for a particular web application on the SharePoint farm.

Solution: Use the `Set-SPWorkflowConfig` cmdlet.

The `Set-SPWorkflowConfig` cmdlet enables you to modify the workflow configuration settings for a specific web application or site collection. Each setting, listed here, is a Boolean parameter:

▶ `DeclarativeWorkflowsEnabled`

▶ `EmailNoPermissionParticipantsEnabled`

▶ `SendDocumentToExternalParticipants`

Listing 4.20 shows a sample modification command line for a web application. Listing 4.21 illustrates modification of the site collection workflow configuration.

LISTING 4.20 **Modifying the Workflow Settings for a Web Application**

```
Set-SPWorkflowConfig -WebApplication "SharePoint - 80"
-DeclarativeWorkflowsEnabled:$true
-EmailNoPermissionParticipantsEnabled:$false
-SendDocumentToExternalParticipants:$false
```

LISTING 4.21 **Modifying the Workflow Settings for a Site Collection**

```
Set-SPWorkflowConfig -SiteCollection "http://sp2013"
-DeclarativeWorkflowsEnabled:$true
-EmailNoPermissionParticipantsEnabled:$false
-SendDocumentToExternalParticipants:$false
```

TIP Use `Get-SPWorkflowConfig` to validate the modifications. The site collection output only displays the `DeclarativeWorkflowEnabled` setting.

The `DeclarativeWorkflowEnabled` parameter determines whether users can define workflows from deployed managed code. The default value is `True`.

The `EmailNoPermissionParticipantsEnabled` parameter determines whether a user who does not have permissions to the site should receive an e-mail if a task is assigned to him or her. The default value is `True`.

The `SendDocumentToExternalParticipants` parameter specifies whether external users should receive a copy of the workflow document. The default value is `False`.

These parameters correspond, respectively, to the workflow settings available in Central Administration, as shown in Figure 4.6.

FIGURE 4.6 Workflow settings for a web application in Central Administration.

Display Available Timer Jobs on the Farm

Scenario/Problem: You need to obtain a timer jobs reference and therefore need a listing of available timer jobs.

Solution: Use the `Get-SPTimerJob` cmdlet without any parameters to retrieve all available timer jobs.

To obtain a timer job reference object, you need to find the identity of the timer job. Using `Get-SPTimerJob` by itself (see Listing 4.22) displays all available timer jobs, as shown in Figure 4.7.

LISTING 4.22 **Displaying All Available Timer Jobs**

```
Get-SPTimerJob
```

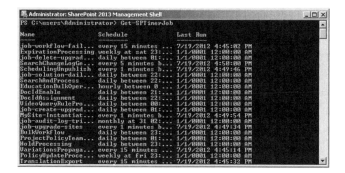

FIGURE 4.7 `Get-SPTimerJob` displays all available timer jobs.

Get a Specific Timer Job

Scenario/Problem: You need to obtain a specific timer job reference.

Solution: Use the `Get-SPTimerJob` cmdlet to assign a variable the results using the `-Identity` parameter.

Providing the identity of the timer job with the `Get-SPTimerJob` cmdlet retrieves a specific timer job. Use this to assign the results to an object for use in other cmdlets, as shown in Listing 4.23.

LISTING 4.23 **Assigning a Variable to a Specific Timer Job**

```
$timerJob = Get-SPTimerJob -Identity "DocIDEnable"
```

In this case, the `Identity` parameter is the name shown when retrieving all timer jobs (`Get-SPTimerJob`). You also can use the GUID of the timer job.

Enable a Timer Job

Scenario/Problem: You want to enable a specific timer job.

Solution: Use the `Enable-SPTimerJob` cmdlet.

To enable a timer job, execute the `Enable-SPTimerJob` cmdlet with the `Identity` of the timer job or a timer job variable. Listing 4.24 shows a sample command line.

LISTING 4.24 **Enabling a Timer Job**

```
$timerJob = Get-SPTimerJob -Identity "DocIDEnable"
Enable-SPTimerJob $timerJob
```

Disable a Timer Job

Scenario/Problem: You want to disable a specific timer job.

Solution: Use the `Disable-SPTimerJob` cmdlet.

To disable a timer job, execute the `Disable-SPTimerJob` cmdlet with the `Identity` of the timer job or a timer job variable. Listing 4.25 shows a sample command line.

LISTING 4.25 **Disabling a Timer Job**

```
$timerJob = Get-SPTimerJob -Identity "DocIDEnable"
Disable-SPTimerJob $timerJob
```

Start a Timer Job

Scenario/Problem: You want to start a specific timer job.

Solution: Use the `Start-SPTimerJob` cmdlet.

To start a timer job, execute the `Start-SPTimerJob` cmdlet with the `Identity` of the timer job or a timer job variable. Listing 4.26 shows a sample command line.

LISTING 4.26 **Starting a Timer Job**

```
$timerJob = Get-SPTimerJob -Identity "DocIDEnable"
Start-SPTimerJob $timerJob
```

In this scenario, the timer job kicks off when you start it manually. This is the same as selecting the Run Now button in Central Administration.

> **TIP** You cannot start a timer job that is disabled. Use `Enable-SPTimerJob` first to ensure that the timer job is enabled before attempting to start the job.

Set the Schedule for a Timer Job

> **Scenario/Problem:** You need to set or modify the schedule of a specific timer job.

Solution: Use the `Set-SPTimerJob` cmdlet.

Setting the schedule for a timer job can be facilitated by using the `Set-SPTimerJob` cmdlet. Execute the `Start-SPTimerJob` cmdlet with the `Identity` of the timer job or a timer job variable along with the `Schedule` parameter. Listing 4.27 shows a sample command line.

LISTING 4.27 **Setting the Schedule for a Timer Job**

```
$timerJob = Get-SPTimerJob -Identity "DocIDEnable"
Set-SPTimerJob -Identity $timerJob -Schedule "Daily at 18:00:00"
```

The `Schedule` parameter is a string value but must conform to one of the following schedule string formats:

- Every X minutes between 0 and 59.
- Hourly between 0 and 59.
- Daily at `hh:mm:ss`.
- Weekly between `<day>` `hh:mm:ss` and `<day>` `hh:mm:ss`. (`<day>` is the three-letter day of the week: `Sun`, `Mon`, `Tue`, `Wed`, `Thu`, `Fri`, or `Sat`.)
- Monthly at `dd` `hh:mm:ss`.
- Yearly at `<month>` `dd` `hh:mm:ss`. (`<month>` is the three-letter month: `Jan`, `Feb`, `Mar`, and so on.)

CHAPTER 5

Web Application Management

This chapter outlines the SharePoint PowerShell commands that you use to manage the web applications within your SharePoint farm.

Display Available Web Applications on the Farm

Scenario/Problem: You need to obtain a web application reference and therefore need a listing of available web applications.

Solution: Use the `Get-SPWebApplication` cmdlet without any parameters to retrieve all available web applications.

To obtain a web application reference object, you need to find the identity of the web application. Using the `Get-SPWebApplication` by itself (see Listing 5.1) displays all available web applications, as shown in Figure 5.1.

LISTING 5.1 **Display All Available Web Applications**

```
Get-SPWebApplication
```

FIGURE 5.1 `Get-SPWebApplication` displays all available web applications.

Get a Specific Web Application

Scenario/Problem: You need to obtain a specific web application reference.

Solution: Use the `Get-SPWebApplication` cmdlet to assign a variable to the results using the `-Identity` parameter.

Providing the identity of the web application with the `Get-SPWebApplication` cmdlet retrieves a specific web application. Use this to assign the results to an object for use in other cmdlets, as shown in Listing 5.2.

LISTING 5.2 **Assigning a Variable to a Specific Web Application**

```
$webApp = Get-SPWebApplication -Identity "PSWebApp"
```

`Identity`, in this case, can be the display name shown when retrieving all web applications (`Get-SPWebApplication`). You can also use the URL instead.

Remove a Web Application

Scenario/Problem: You need to remove a web application from the current server configuration.

Solution: Use the `Remove-SPWebApplication` cmdlet with a web application variable.

The `Remove-SPWebApplication` cmdlet enables you to remove a specific web application from the current server. Use this in conjunction with the `Get-SPWebApplication` cmdlet (explained in a previous section), as shown in Listing 5.3, or just use the web application identity directly in line, as shown in Listing 5.4.

LISTING 5.3 **Removing a Web Application Using a Variable Example**

```
$webApp = Get-SPWebApplication -Identity "PSWebApp"
Remove-SPWebApplication $webApp
```

LISTING 5.4 **Removing a Web Application Directly**

```
Remove-SPWebApplication -Identity "PSWebApp"
```

TIP You can also remove the underlying database(s) and data by using the —RemoveContentDatabases switch parameter. Use this only if you are no longer using the web application at all on the farm.

Create a New Web Application

Scenario/Problem: You need to create a new web application.

Solution: Use the `New-SPWebApplication` cmdlet.

To add a new web application, use the `New-SPWebApplication` cmdlet, as follows:

```
New-SPWebApplication -applicationpool <name of new application pool> -
name <name of new web app> -applicationpoolaccount <service account to
be used for the application pool> -port <desired port number>
```

Listing 5.5 shows an example command-line entry for creating the main SharePoint web application.

LISTING 5.5 **Creating a New Web Application**

```
New-SPWebApplication -applicationpool NewWebApp -name NewWebApp
-applicationpoolaccount SP\AppPoolAccount -port 80
```

This process might take a few minutes. After it completes, the display name and the URL of the new web application appear in the console.

TIP If you do not include the port number, a random port number is assigned. The first web application created uses port 80.

Configure Web Application Settings

Scenario/Problem: You need to modify settings of a web application.

Solution: Use the `Set-SPWebApplication` cmdlet with a web application variable.

The `Set-SPWebApplication` has several parameter sets for configuring various settings on the web application. Running `Set-SPWebApplication` with the `-?` parameter displays each parameter set, as in Figure 5.2.

Use the first parameter set to configure the default quota template, the default time zone, and/or the service application proxy group. Use the second parameter set to configure the zone of the web application, along with the associated authentication settings. Finally, use the third parameter set to configure various e-mail settings for the web application.

FIGURE 5.2 `Set-SPWebApplication` has three different parameter sets.

Extend a Web Application

Scenario/Problem: You need to extend a web application to a new zone.

Solution: Use the `New-SPWebApplicationExtension` cmdlet.

If you need to extend a web application to a different zone, that zone must not already be in use. `New-SPWebApplicationExtension` requires only the web application identity, the name of the new website that will extend the web application, and the zone. However, it is a good idea to include the new URL and `HostHeader` that the web application extension will use for the zone. Listing 5.6 shows an example command-line entry for extending the main SharePoint web application.

LISTING 5.6 **Extending a Web Application Example**

```
New-SPWebApplicationExtension -Identity "SharePoint - 80" -Name "SP
Internet Site" -Zone Internet -Url "http://internet" -HostHeader
"http://internet.sp2013.com"
```

The URL is the public-facing HTTP address; the `HostHeader` entry is the internal alternate access mapping. The `Zone` parameter can be one of the following:

- ▶ Default
- ▶ Intranet
- ▶ Internet
- ▶ Extranet
- ▶ Custom

The zone used in the command must not already be used. That is, a web application cannot already be extended to that zone.

> **TIP** A handful of optional parameters can be used to configure security and authentication.

Create an Alternate Access-Mapping URL

> **Scenario/Problem:** You need to create a new alternate access mapping for a web application.

Solution: Use the `New-SPAlternateURL` cmdlet.

You can programmatically generate alternate access mappings using the `New-SPAlternateURL` cmdlet. The main parameter set requires the URL and the web application name, as Listing 5.7 shows.

LISTING 5.7 **Creating an Alternate Access Mapping**

```
New-SPAlternateURL -URL "http://intranet.sp2013.com" -WebApplication
"SharePoint - 80" -Internal -Zone Intranet
```

Using the `-Internal` switch parameter creates the mapping for internal use. Omitting this parameter generates a public URL entry. Use the `-Zone` parameter to specify the zone. The valid values follow:

- ▶ Default
- ▶ Intranet
- ▶ Internet
- ▶ Extranet
- ▶ Custom

> **TIP** For external resources, use the second parameter set which requires the external resource name (`-ResourceName`) instead of the web application.

Display All Alternate Access Mappings

Scenario/Problem: You need to obtain an alternate access mapping reference and therefore need a listing of available alternate URLs.

Solution: Use the `Get-SPAlternateURL` cmdlet without any parameters.

To obtain a reference variable, you need to find the identity of the URL. Using `Get-SPAlternateURL` without any parameters, as shown in Listing 5.8, displays the current URL mappings.

LISTING 5.8 **Example Command to Display All Alternate URLs**

```
Get-SPAlternateURL
```

Get a Specific Alternate URL Entry

Scenario/Problem: You need to obtain a specific alternate URL reference.

Solution: Use the `Get-SPAlternateURL` cmdlet using the `-Identity` parameter, and assign a variable the results.

Providing the identity of the alternate URL with the `Get-SPDatabase` cmdlet retrieves a specific alternate access-mapping instance. Use this to assign the results to a variable for use in other cmdlets, as shown in Listing 5.9.

LISTING 5.9 **Assigning a Variable to a Specific Alternate URL Entry**

```
$altURL = Get-SPAlternateURL -Identity "http://intranet.sp2013.com"
```

The `Identity` parameter is the incoming URL address for the specific alternate access mapping.

Change the Zone of an Alternate Access Mapping

Scenario/Problem: You need to change the zone of an existing alternate access mapping.

Solution: Use the `Set-SPAlternateURL` cmdlet.

The `Set-SPAlternateURL` enables you to modify the zone. This is the only setting that you can modify using the cmdlet. The `-Zone` parameter can be one of the following:

- ▶ `Default`
- ▶ `Intranet`
- ▶ `Internet`
- ▶ `Extranet`
- ▶ `Custom`

Listing 5.10 shows an example command line.

LISTING 5.10 **Changing the Zone of an Alternate Access Mapping**

```
Set-SPAlternateURL -Identity "http://intranet.sp2013.com" -Zone Intranet
```

The `-Identity` parameter can be the incoming URL or a variable identifying the alternate access mapping (using the `Get-SPAlternateURL` cmdlet).

> **NOTE** If the alternate access mapping entry is public and the zone is Default, you may not change the zone until another public entry is created for the Default zone.

Remove an Alternate Access Mapping

> **Scenario/Problem:** You need to remove an existing alternate access mapping entry.

Solution: Use the `Remove-SPAlternateURL` cmdlet.

The `Remove-SPAlternateURL` cmdlet enables you to remove the specified alternate URL entry. The only required parameter is the `Identity` of the URL mapping, as shown in Listing 5.11.

LISTING 5.11 **Remove an Existing Alternate Access Mapping**

```
Remove-SPAlternateURL -Identity "http://intranet.sp2013.com"
```

The `-Identity` parameter can be the incoming URL or a variable identifying the alternate access mapping (using the `Get-SPAlternateURL` cmdlet).

> **NOTE** If the alternate access mapping entry is public and the zone is Default, you may not remove the alternate URL entry.

CHAPTER 6

Service Application Management

This chapter outlines the SharePoint PowerShell commands that manage the service applications within your SharePoint farm. Service applications are extensions of functionality within SharePoint and can be scaled across servers (depending on the architecture topology). Some service applications support spanning across farms (cross-farm services). The cmdlets in this chapter are generic; later chapters, contained in Part IV and Part V, describe specific service application cmdlets and configuration options.

Install Service Applications

> **Scenario/Problem:** You need to install all service applications to the farm using a script.

Solution: Use the `Install-SPService` cmdlet with the `-Provision` switch parameter.

Using the `Install-SPService` cmdlet installs all service applications on a server based on the services, service proxies, and service instances stored in the local registry. Using the `-Provision` switch parameter allows the service applications to be installed using the default settings. Listing 6.1 shows an example command line.

LISTING 6.1 **Installing All Available Service Applications**

```
Install-SPService -Provision
```

Display Available Service Applications on the Farm

> **Scenario/Problem:** You need to obtain a service application reference and therefore need a listing of available service applications.

Solution: Use the `Get-SPServiceApplication` cmdlet without any parameters to retrieve all available service applications.

To obtain a service application reference object, you need to find the identity of the service application. Using the `Get-SPServiceApplication` by itself (see Listing 6.2) displays all available service applications, as shown in Figure 6.1.

LISTING 6.2 **Displaying All Available Service Applications**

```
Get-SPServiceApplication
```

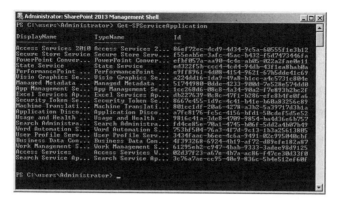

FIGURE 6.1 `Get-SPServiceApplication` displays all available service applications.

Get a Specific Service Application

Scenario/Problem: You need to obtain a specific service application reference.

Solution: Use the `Get-SPServiceApplication` cmdlet to assign a variable the results using the `-Identity` parameter.

Providing the identity of the service application with the `Get-SPServiceApplication` cmdlet retrieves a specific service application. Use this to assign the results to an object for use in other cmdlets, as shown in Listing 6.3.

LISTING 6.3 **Assigning a Variable to a Specific Service Application**

```
$sApp = Get-SPServiceApplication -Identity bc4399ed-a
2e0-4397-bf07-cd3d207e630e
```

TIP Instead of using `-Identity`, you can use `-Name` and provide the name of the service application in quotes.

Configure IIS Settings for a Service Application

Scenario/Problem: You need to configure IIS settings for a service application.

Solution: Use the `Set-SPServiceApplication` cmdlet to set IIS settings using a service application variable.

The `Set-SPServiceApplication` cmdlet enables you to set the default endpoint, the application pool, and/or the service proxy for a specific service application. Use this in conjunction with the `Get-SPServiceApplication` cmdlet (explained in the previous section), as shown in Listing 6.4.

LISTING 6.4 **Example Configuration Script for a Service Application**

```
$sApp = Get-SPServiceApplication -Identity bc4399ed-a
2e0-4397-bf07-cd3d207e630e
Set-SPServiceApplication $sApp -IISWebServiceApplicationPool
"ServiceAppPool"
```

The main configuration parameters are:

- ▶ `DefaultEndPoint`
- ▶ `IISWebServiceApplicationPool`
- ▶ `ServiceApplicationProxyGroup`

> **TIP** Use the `Get-SPServiceApplicationEndPoint` to create an object to pass into the `-DefaultEndPoint` parameter. The example in Help that uses `https` does not work.

> **TIP** the `Get-SPServiceApplicationProxyGroup` to create an object to pass into the `-ServiceApplicationProxyGroup` parameter.

Share a Service Application

> **Scenario/Problem:** You need to make a service application available outside of the local farm.

Solution: Use the `Publish-SPServiceApplication` cmdlet with a service application variable.

The `Publish-SPServiceApplication` cmdlet enables you to make a specific service application available outside the current farm. Use this in conjunction with the `Get-SPServiceApplication` cmdlet (explained in a previous section), as shown in Listing 6.5.

LISTING 6.5 **Example Configuration Script for Sharing a Service Application**

```
$sApp = Get-SPServiceApplication -Identity bc4399ed-a
2e0-4397-bf07-cd3d207e630e
Publish-SPServiceApplication $sApp
```

> **TIP** You can provide a help page link (URL) using the -Infolink parameter with the Publish-SPServiceApplication cmdlet.

> **TIP** To stop sharing a service application use UnPublish-SPServiceApplication.

Remove a Service Application

Scenario/Problem: You need to remove a service application from the current server configuration.

Solution: Use the Remove-SPServiceApplication cmdlet with a service application variable.

The Remove-SPServiceApplication cmdlet enables you to remove a specific service application from the current server. Use this in conjunction with the Get-SPServiceApplication cmdlet (explained in a previous section), as shown in Listing 6.6.

LISTING 6.6 **Example Configuration Script for Removing a Service Application**

```
$sApp = Get-SPServiceApplication -Identity bc4399ed-a
2e0-4397-bf07-cd3d207e630e
Remove-SPServiceApplication $sApp
```

> **TIP** You may also remove the underlying database and data by using the -RemoveData switch parameter. Only use this if you are no longer using the service application on the farm.

Display Service Instances on a Server

Scenario/Problem: You need to obtain a service instance reference and therefore need a listing of available service instances.

Solution: Use the Get-SPServiceInstance cmdlet with the Server parameter to display all the service instances on that server.

To obtain a service instance reference object, you need to find the identity of the service instance. Using the Get-SPServiceInstance with the Server parameter (see Listing 6.7) displays all available service applications, as shown in Figure 6.2.

LISTING 6.7 Displaying All Available Service Instances Example

```
Get-SPServiceInstance -Server sp2013svr01 -All
```

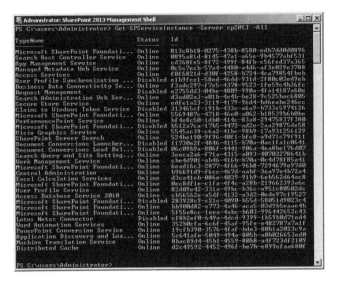

FIGURE 6.2 `Get-SPServiceInstance` displays all service instances on the specified server.

> **TIP** Running the `Get-SPServiceInstance` cmdlet without the `Server` parameter returns all service instances on the entire farm.

Get a Specific Service Instance

Scenario/Problem: You need to obtain a specific service instance reference.

Solution: Use the `Get-SPServiceInstance` cmdlet to assign a variable to the results using the `-Identity` parameter.

Providing the identity of the service instance with the `Get-SPServiceInstance` cmdlet retrieves a specific service instance. Use this to assign the results to an object for use in other cmdlets, as shown in Listing 6.8.

LISTING 6.8 Assigning a Variable to a Specific Service Instance

```
$serviceInst = Get-SPServiceInstance -Identity 5fedc699-7810-4157-9c59-
19f7d6e67e38
```

Start a Service Instance

Scenario/Problem: You need to start a specific service instance.

Solution: Use the `Get-SPServiceInstance` cmdlet to assign a variable the results using the `-Identity` parameter, and then use `Start-SPServiceInstance` using that variable.

The `Start-SPServiceInstance` cmdlet starts the specified service on the current server. You can provide the identity directly to the cmdlet or use a variable, as shown in Listing 6.9.

LISTING 6.9 **Starting a Service Instance**

```
$serviceInst = Get-SPServiceInstance -Identity 5fedc699-7810-4157-9c59-
19f7d6e67e38
Start-SPServiceInstance $serviceInst
```

Stop a Service Instance

Scenario/Problem: You need to stop a specific service instance.

Solution: Use the `Get-SPServiceInstance` cmdlet to assign a variable to the results using the `-Identity` parameter, and then use `Stop-SPServiceInstance` using that variable.

The `Stop-SPServiceInstance` cmdlet stops the specified service on the current server. You can provide the identity directly to the cmdlet or use a variable, as shown in Listing 6.10.

LISTING 6.10 **Stopping a Service Instance**

```
$serviceInst = Get-SPServiceInstance -Identity 5fedc699-7810-4157-9c59-
19f7d6e67e38
Stop-SPServiceInstance $serviceInst
```

Ancillary Cmdlets for Service Applications

Scenario/Problem: You need to create instances of service application items for use within other cmdlets covered in this chapter.

Solution: Use the cmdlets listed in this section to obtain various instances.

This chapter covers the basic or more common cmdlets. For more advance scripting with service applications, the following cmdlets nouns are available:

▶ SPServiceApplicationProxy

▶ SPServiceApplicationProxyGroup

▶ UniquePermissions SPServiceApplicationSecurity

▶ SPServiceContext

▶ UseParentTopNav SPServiceApplicationEndPoint

CHAPTER 7

SharePoint Database Management

This chapter outlines the SharePoint PowerShell commands that manage the underlying SharePoint databases. It explains the cmdlets to create and remove databases, along with several backup and restore operations.

Display All SharePoint Databases

Scenario/Problem: You need to obtain a service application reference and therefore need a listing of available service applications.

Solution: Use the `Get-SPDatabase` cmdlet with the `ServerInstance` parameter to retrieve all available databases.

To obtain a database reference object, you need to find the identity of the database. Using the `Get-SPDatabase` cmdlet with the `ServerInstance` parameter (see Listing 7.1) displays all available databases, as shown in Figure 7.1.

You need to pass in the SQL Server instance to the `ServerInstance` parameter. This is not any of the SharePoint servers.

LISTING 7.1 **Sample Command to Display All Databases**

```
Get-SPDatabase -ServerInstance "SP2013\SQLSharePoint"
```

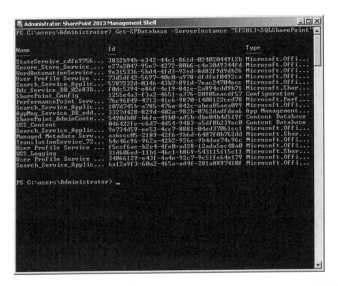

FIGURE 7.1 The `Get-SPDatabase -ServerInstance` cmdlet displays all databases on the SQL Server.

Get a Specific Database

Scenario/Problem: You need to obtain a specific database reference.

Solution: Use the `Get-SPDatabase` cmdlet using the `-Identity` parameter to assign a variable to the results.

Providing the identity of the database with the `Get-SPDatabase` cmdlet retrieves a specific database. Use this to assign the results to an object for use in other cmdlets, as shown in Listing 7.2.

LISTING 7.2 **Assigning a Variable to a Specific Database**

```
$database = Get-SPDatabase
-Identity 47036154-7a05-44be-9137-9be09f43ccb5
```

Create a New Content Database

Scenario/Problem: You want to create a new content database and associate it to an existing web application.

Solution: Use the `New-SPContentDatabase`

The `New-SPContentDatabase` cmdlet enables you to create a new content database using the `Name` parameter for the name and using the `WebApplication` parameter to associate it to the specified web application. Because you can use the name of the web application, you do not need to obtain the actual identity. Listing 7.3 shows a sample command-line entry.

LISTING 7.3 **Creating a New Content Database Example**

```
New-SPContentDatabase -Name NewContentDB -WebApplication "PSWebApp"
```

Creating the new content database takes a moment. An output of the content database information confirms the creation, as shown in Figure 7.2.

TIP Use the `Get-SPWebApplication` cmdlet to list out the names of the web applications.

FIGURE 7.2 Content database information is displayed after creation.

Display All Content Databases for a Web Application

Scenario/Problem: You want to see all content databases associated to a specific web application.

Solution: Use the `Get-SPContentDatabase` cmdlet with the `WebApplication` parameter.

The `Get-SPContentDatabase` cmdlet has several parameter sets. One set enables a `WebApplication` parameter to be used. Using the `WebApplication` parameter with the `Get-SPContentDatabase` cmdlet (see Listing 7.4) displays information about all content databases associated to the specified web application, as shown in Figure 7.3.

LISTING 7.4 **Displaying All Content Databases**

```
Get-SPContentDatabase -WebApplication "PSWebApp"
```

FIGURE 7.3 Results of using the `Get-SPContentDatabase` cmdlet with the `WebApplication` parameter.

> **TIP** Use the `Get-SPContentDatabase` cmdlet with the `Identity` parameter to assign the specific content database reference to a variable for use in other cmdlets.

Detach a Content Database from a Web Application

> **Scenario/Problem:** You need to dissociate a content database from a web application without removing the database or deleting the data.

Solution: Use the `Dismount-SPContentDatabase` cmdlet with a content database variable.

The `Dismount-SPContentDatabase` cmdlet enables you to dissociate the specified content database with the web application without removing the underlying database itself. Use this in conjunction with the `Get-SPContentDatabase` cmdlet, as shown in Listing 7.5.

> **TIP** Use the `Get-SPContentDatabase` cmdlet with the `WebApplication` parameter to confirm that the content database was dismounted from the web application.

LISTING 7.5 **Sample Script for Dismounting a Content Database**

```
$database = Get-SPContentDatabase
-Identity 025b1239-cd62-451e-943d-dff2e0d52ec8
Dismount-SPContentDatabase $database
```

Attach a Content Database to a Web Application

> **Scenario/Problem:** You need to associate a content database to a web application.

Solution: Use the `Mount-SPContentDatabase` cmdlet with the `WebApplication` parameter.

The `Mount-SPContentDatabase` cmdlet enables you to associate the specified content database with a web application. The command-line entry is similar to the process of creating a new content database because the parameters are `Name` and `WebApplication`, as shown in Listing 7.6.

LISTING 7.6 **Sample Script for Mounting a Content Database**

```
Mount-SPContentDatabase -Name "NewContentDB"
-WebApplication "PSWebApp"
```

A confirmation listing of the content database information displays, just as in creating a new content database.

Delete a Content Database

Scenario/Problem: You want to remove a content database from its web application and delete the actual SQL Server database and data.

Solution: Use the `Remove-SPContentDatabase` cmdlet with a database variable.

The `Remove-SPContentDatabase` cmdlet enables you to delete the specified content database. Use this in conjunction with the `Get-SPContentDatabase` cmdlet, as shown in Listing 7.7.

LISTING 7.7 **Sample Script for Removing a Content Database**

```
$database = Get-SPContentDatabase
-Identity 025b1239-cd62-451e-943d-dff2e0d52ec8
Remove-SPContentDatabase $database
```

TIP Instead of using the database variable, you can execute `Remove-SPContentDatabase` by just providing the name of the content database without any parameter entries (for example, `Remove-SPContentDatabase "NewContentDB"`).

Create a New Configuration Database

Scenario/Problem: You want to create a new configuration database.

Solution: Use the `New-SPConfigurationDatabase` cmdlet to create a new configuration database and associate it to the specified web application.

The `New-SPConfigurationDatabase` cmdlet enables you to create a new configuration database using the `DatabaseName` and `DatabaseServer` parameters. Listing 7.8 shows a sample command-line entry.

LISTING 7.8 **Creating a New Configuration Database**

```
New-SPConfigurationDatabase -DatabaseName NewConfigurationDB
-DatabaseServer "SP2013\SQLSharePoint"
```

> **NOTE** If the current server is already joined to an existing farm, you cannot create a new configuration database. Use the `Disconnect-SPConfigurationDatabase` cmdlet first to disconnect the current server from the farm.

You need the farm credentials and a passphrase to execute this cmdlet. If you do not provide these in line with the cmdlet, you are prompted to provide this information.

Delete a Configuration Database

> **Scenario/Problem:** You want to remove a configuration database from the farm and delete the actual SQL Server database and data.

Solution: Use the `Remove-SPConfigurationDatabase` cmdlet.

The `Remove-SPConfigurationDatabase` cmdlet enables you to delete the current configuration database. You do not need to pass any parameters into this cmdlet, as shown in Listing 7.9.

LISTING 7.9 **Sample Script for Removing a Configuration Database**

```
Remove-SPConfigurationDatabase
```

> **TIP** Run the `Remove-SPConfigurationDatabase` cmdlet with the `-WhatIf` switch parameter to display the actual configuration database that will be removed.

This cmdlet already knows which configuration database the current server and SharePoint farm are using.

Back Up a Configuration Database

> **Scenario/Problem:** You want to back up a configuration database within your SQL Server.

Solution: Use the `Backup-SPConfigurationDatabase` cmdlet with the `Directory` parameter.

The `Backup-SPConfigurationDatabase` cmdlet enables you to perform a backup on a configuration database, placing the backup files in the directory specified. Listing 7.10 shows an example.

LISTING 7.10 Sample Script for Backing Up a Configuration Database

```
Backup-SPConfigurationDatabase -Directory F:\Backups
```

This cmdlet already knows which configuration database the current server and SharePoint farm are using. Use the `-DatabaseServer` and `-DatabaseName` parameters to specify the actual configuration database name and location.

If you are backing up the current configuration database the farm is using, you also can use the `Backup-SPFarm` cmdlet with the `ConfigurationOnly` switch parameter, as shown in Listing 7.11.

LISTING 7.11 Using `Backup-SPFarm` to Back Up the Configuration Database

```
Backup-SPFarm -BackupMethod Full -Directory F:\Backups
-ConfigurationOnly
```

> **TIP** For backup and restore operations of the current farm, using the `Backup-SPFarm` cmdlet with the `ConfigurationOnly` switch parameter is recommended to back up the configuration database.

The `BackupMethod` parameter can be either `Full` or `Differential`. `Full` backs up the entire configuration, whereas `Differential` backs up only changes that have occurred since the last full backup was performed.

Restore a Configuration Database

> **Scenario/Problem:** You want to restore a configuration database from a backup.

Solution: Use the `Restore-SPFarm` cmdlet with the `Directory` parameter and `ConfigurationOnly` switch parameter.

The `Restore-SPFarm` cmdlet enables you to restore a configuration database based on the backup files in the directory specified. Use the `-ConfigurationOnly` switch parameter to restore only the configuration database, as shown in Listing 7.12.

LISTING 7.12 Sample Script for Restoring a Configuration Database

```
Restore-SPFarm -Directory F:\Backups -ConfigurationOnly
-RestoreMethod Overwrite
```

The RestoreMethod parameter can be New or Overwrite. Using New creates a new location for the backup to be restored. Overwrite will restore the backup in place and overwrite the current configuration.

Back Up the SharePoint Farm

Scenario/Problem: You want to back up the entire farm.

Solution: Use the Backup-SPFarm cmdlet with the Directory parameter.

The Backup-SPFarm cmdlet enables you to perform a backup of the entire farm (or item in the farm), placing the backup files in the directory specified. Listing 7.13 shows an example.

LISTING 7.13 **Sample Script for Backing Up the SharePoint Farm**

```
Backup-SPFarm -BackupMethod Full -Directory F:\Backups
```

The BackupMethod parameter can be either Full or Differential. Full backs up the entire configuration, whereas Differential backs up only changes that have occurred since the last full backup was performed.

TIP Run Backup-SPFarm with the -ShowTree parameter to display all items in the farm that can be backed up. Use the -Item parameter with Backup-SPFarm to back up a specific item in the farm.

Restore the SharePoint Farm

Scenario/Problem: You want to restore the farm from a backup.

Solution: Use the Restore-SPFarm cmdlet with the Directory parameter.

The Restore-SPFarm cmdlet enables you to restore the farm based on the backup files in the directory specified, as shown in Listing 7.14.

LISTING 7.14 **Sample Script for Restoring a Farm**

```
Restore-SPFarm -Directory F:\Backups -RestoreMethod Overwrite
```

The RestoreMethod parameter can be New or Overwrite. Using New creates a new location for the backup to be restored. Overwrite restores the backup in place and overwrites the current farm content.

> **TIP** Use the –Item parameter with the `Restore-SPFarm` cmdlet to restore a specific item in the farm.

Back Up a Site Collection

> **Scenario/Problem:** You want to back up a specific site collection.

Solution: Use the `Backup-SPSite` cmdlet.

The `Backup-SPSite` cmdlet enables you to perform a backup of a specific site collection, creating a backup file based on the path specified. Listing 7.15 shows an example.

LISTING 7.15 **Sample Script for Backing Up a Site Collection**

```
Backup-SPSite -Identity "http://sp2013/sites/BICenter"
-Path F:\Backups\BICenter.bak
```

The `Identity` parameter can be the URL or the GUID of the site collection. Using the URL is usually easier. The `Path` parameter defines where the backup will be stored, along with the name of the backup file to create.

> **TIP** Run `Get-SPSite` without any parameters to list the available site collections.

Restore a Site Collection

> **Scenario/Problem:** You want to restore a site collection from a backup.

Solution: Use the `Restore-SPSite` cmdlet.

The `Restore-SPSite` cmdlet enables you to restore a site collection based on the backup file in the path specified, as shown in Listing 7.16.

LISTING 7.16 **Sample Script for Restoring a Site Collection**

```
Restore-SPSite -Identity "http://sp2013/sites/BICenter"
-Path F:\Backups\BICenter.bak -Force
```

The `Force` switch parameter is needed to overwrite an existing site collection. You also specify can the `DatabaseName` and `DatabaseServer` parameters to tell where the content of the site collection should be stored.

CHAPTER 8

Site Management

This chapter outlines the SharePoint PowerShell commands used to manage the site collections and sites within your SharePoint farm.

Display All Available Site Collections on the Farm

Scenario/Problem: You need to obtain a site collection reference and therefore need a listing of available site collection URLs.

Solution: Use the `Get-SPSite` cmdlet without any parameters to retrieve all available site collections.

To obtain a site collection reference object, you need to find the URL (`Identity`) of the site collection. Using the `Get-SPSite` cmdlet by itself (see Listing 8.1) displays all available site collections, as shown in Figure 8.1.

LISTING 8.1 **Displaying All Available Site Collections**

```
Get-SPSite
```

FIGURE 8.1 The `Get-SPSite` cmdlet displays all available sites.

Display Available Site Collections in a Web Application

Scenario/Problem: You need to obtain a site collection reference and therefore need a listing of available site collection URLs within a specific web application.

Solution: Use the `Get-SPSite` cmdlet with the `WebApplication` parameter.

To obtain a site collection reference object, you need to find the URL (Identity) of the site collection. Using the Get-SPSite cmdlet with the WebApplication parameter, as shown in Listing 8.2, displays all available site collections in the specified web application.

LISTING 8.2 **Displaying Available Site Collections in a Web Application**

```
Get-SPSite -WebApplication "SharePoint - 80"
```

Display Available Site Collections in a Content Database

Scenario/Problem: You need to obtain a site collection reference and therefore need a listing of available site collection URLs.

Solution: Use the Get-SPSite cmdlet with the ContentDatabase parameter.

To obtain a site collection reference object, you need to find the URL (Identity) of the site collection. Using the Get-SPSite cmdlet with the ContentDatabase parameter, as shown in Listing 8.3, displays all available site collections in the specified content database.

LISTING 8.3 **Displaying Available Site Collections in a Content Database**

```
Get-SPSite -ContentDatabase "WSS_CONTENT1"
```

TIP Use the SP-GetContentDatabase cmdlet to display the available content databases used by the SharePoint farm.

Get a Specific Site Collection

Scenario/Problem: You need to obtain a specific site collection reference.

Solution: Use the Get-SPSite cmdlet to assign a variable the results using the -Identity parameter.

Providing the identity of the site collection with the Get-SPSite cmdlet retrieves a specific site collection. Use this to assign the results to an object for use in other cmdlets, as shown in Listing 8.4.

LISTING 8.4 **Assigning a Variable to a Specific Site Collection**

```
$siteCol = Get-SPSite -Identity "http://sp2013"
```

Remove a Site Collection

Scenario/Problem: You need to remove a site collection from your SharePoint farm.

Solution: Use the Remove-SPSite cmdlet with a site collection variable.

The Remove-SPSite cmdlet enables you to remove a specific site collection from the current server. Use this in conjunction with the Get-SPSite cmdlet (explained in a previous section), as shown in Listing 8.5, or just use the site collection identity directly in line, as shown in Listing 8.6.

LISTING 8.5 **Removing a Site Collection Using a Variable**

```
$siteCol = Get-SPSite -Identity "http://sp2013/sites/sitecol"
Remove-SPSite $siteCol
```

LISTING 8.6 **Removing a Site Collection Directly**

```
Remove-SPSite -Identity "http://sp2013/sites/sitecol"
```

The Remove-SPSite cmdlet has an optional switch parameter named GradualDelete. Using this parameter gradually removes the site collection and any subsites underneath. This helps keeps the SharePoint load down and, therefore, is highly recommended for large site collections.

NOTE There is also a switch parameter for Remove-SPSite that removes Active Directory accounts. The parameter is named DeleteADAccounts. This can be dangerous and therefore it is recommended to not use this switch parameter.

Create a Site Collection

Scenario/Problem: You need to create a new site collection.

Solution: Use the New-SPSite cmdlet.

To add a new site collection, use the `New-SPSite` cmdlet as follows:

```
New-SPSite -url <full url of new site collection>
-name <name of new site collection>
-owneralias <site collection administrator>
-template <site collection template to use>
```

Listing 8.7 shows a sample command-line entry for creating the root site collection using the Team Site template.

LISTING 8.7 **Creating a New Site Collection**

```
New-SPSite -url http://sp2013/sites/sitecol -name Home
-owneralias SP\SiteAdmin -template STS#0
```

The site template names can be found using `Get-SPWebTemplate`. If no template is provided, the site collection will still be created. In this case, after the site is accessed via the browser, SharePoint prompts for a site collection template to be selected.

Creating a new site collection using the `New-SPSite` cmdlet might take a few minutes. Afterward the new URL is presented.

> **TIP** You can only create one site collection at the root of the web application. Subsequent site collections must be created using a managed path. See Chapter 4, "Farm Management," for more information on creating a managed path.

Set the Lock State of a Site Collection

Scenario/Problem: You want to allow or prohibit access to the site collection.

Solution: Use the `Set-SPSite` cmdlet with the `LockState` parameter.

The `Set-SPSite` cmdlet has several parameter sets for configuring various settings on the site collection. Running `Set-SPSite` with the `-?` parameter displays each parameter set. The `LockState` parameter enables you to lock or unlock the site collection. The following are valid values for the `LockState` parameter:

- Unlock
- NoAdditions
- ReadOnly
- NoAccess

The Unlock state provides full availability to users (based on the normal permissions). NoAdditions enables you to lock the site collection so that no new content can be added. This does not lock down updates or deletes. To fully lock down the content, use the ReadOnly state. Placing the site collection into the ReadOnly state prevents users from adding, updating, or deleting content. NoAccess disables all access to the site collection. Users will not even be able to navigate to the site collection location (or locations underneath).

Listing 8.8 shows a sample command line for changing the lock state.

LISTING 8.8 **Changing the Lock State of a Site Collection**

```
Set-SPSite -Identity http://sp2013/sites/sitecol -LockState NoAdditions
```

Set the Storage Limits on a Site Collection

Scenario/Problem: You want to modify the storage limitations for a site collection.

Solution: Use the Set-SPSite cmdlet with the MaxSize and WarningSize parameters.

Two parameters work together to set the storage limits on a site collection: MaxSize and WarningSize. Listing 8.9 shows a sample command line for setting the storage limits.

LISTING 8.9 **Setting the Storage Limits on a Site Collection**

```
Set-SPSite -Identity http://sp2013/sites/sitecol -MaxSize 1024
-WarningSize 768
```

Both parameter values are in megabytes. The MaxSize parameter can be any integer value but must be greater than or equal to the WarningSize value. Therefore, the WarningSize parameter can be any value between zero and the MaxSize value.

NOTE You may not be able to set the storage limits if a quota template is being used for the site collection.

Create a Site Under a Site Collection

Scenario/Problem: You want to create sites under your site collection.

Solution: Use the New-SPWeb cmdlet.

To add a new subsite, use the `New-SPWeb` cmdlet as follows:

```
New-SPWeb -url <full url of new site> -name <name of new site>
-template <site template to use>
```

The following switch parameters are available when using the `New-SPWeb` cmdlet:

▶ `AddToTopNav`

▶ `UniquePermissions`

▶ `UseParentTopNav`

The `AddToTopNav` switch parameter places the new site within the top navigation of the site collection. Using the `UseParentTopNav` switch parameter replicates the top nav of the site collection onto the new subsite. Creating a site with `UniquePermissions` forces the site to not inherit permissions from the site collection and grants only the System Account Full Control access.

Listing 8.10 shows a sample command-line entry for creating a subsite using the Team Site template.

LISTING 8.10 **Creating a Site Under a Site Collection**

```
New-SPWeb -url http://sp2013/sites/sitecol/newsubsite
-name "New Sub Site" -template STS#0 -AddToTopNav -UniquePermissions
-UseParentTopNav
```

The site template names can be found using `Get-SPWebTemplate`. If no template is provided, the site still is created. In this case, when the site is accessed via the browser, SharePoint prompts for a site template to be selected.

Display All Subsites Within a Site Collection

Scenario/Problem: You need to obtain a site reference and therefore need a listing of available subsites within a specific site collection.

Solution: Use the `Get-SPWeb` cmdlet with a wildcard `Identity` path.

To display all subsites within a site collection, you need to use the `Get-SPWeb` cmdlet with the `Identity` parameter. If you provide only the site collection URL, `Get-SPWeb` returns only the site collection web object. Therefore, you need to provide a wildcard path, as shown in Listing 8.11.

LISTING 8.11 **Displaying All Subsites Within a Site Collection**

```
Get-SPWeb -Identity "http://sp2013/sites/sitecol/*"
```

You can also use the `Site` parameter instead of the wildcard `Identity` parameter to retrieve all webs, including the site collection web. Listing 8.12 shows a sample command line.

LISTING 8.12 **Displaying All Webs Within a Site Collection**

```
Get-SPWeb -Site "http://sp2013/sites/sitecol"
```

Get a Specific Subsite (Web)

Scenario/Problem: You need to obtain a specific subsite reference.

Solution: Use the `Get-SPWeb` cmdlet to assign a variable the results using the `-Identity` parameter.

Providing the identity of the subsite with the `Get-SPWeb` cmdlet retrieves a specific subsite. Use this to assign the results to an object for use in other cmdlets, as shown in Listing 8.13.

LISTING 8.13 **Assigning a Variable to a Specific Subsite**

```
$web = Get-SPWeb -Identity "http://sp2013/sites/sitecol/subsite"
```

Remove a Subsite (Web) from a Site Collection

Scenario/Problem: You need to remove a subsite from a site collection.

Solution: Use the `Remove-SPWeb` cmdlet.

The `Remove-SPWeb` cmdlet enables you to remove a specific subsite. Use this in conjunction with the `Get-SPWeb` cmdlet (explained in the previous section), as shown in Listing 8.14, or just use the path identity directly in line, as shown in Listing 8.15.

LISTING 8.14 **Removing a Subsite Application Using a Variable**

```
$web = Get-SPWeb -Identity "http://sp2013/sites/sitecol/subsite"
Remove-SPWeb $web
```

LISTING 8.15 **Removing a Subsite Directly**

```
Remove-SPWeb -Identity "http://sp2013/sites/sitecol/subsite"
```

Modify the Subsite (Web) URL

Scenario/Problem: You want to rename the relative URL name for a subsite.

Solution: Use the Set-SPWeb cmdlet with the RelativeURL parameter.

You can easily change the name of the relative URL in which a subsite is accessed by using the Set-SPWeb cmdlet. Provide the URL of the site as the Identity parameter, and use the RelativeURL parameter to provide the new URL, as shown in Listing 8.16.

LISTING 8.16 **Renaming a Subsite**

```
Set-SPWeb -Identity "http://sp2013/sites/sitecol/newsubsite"

-RelativeURL teamsites
```

Notice that the RelativeURL value is not a full URL. The example essentially renames the subsite URL from newsubsite to teamsites. Therefore, after execution, the subsite is accessed by http://sp2013/sites/sitecol/teamsites/.

Move a Site Collection to a Different Content Database

Scenario/Problem: You want to move a particular site collection to a different content database.

Solution: Use the Move-SPSite cmdlet.

The Move-SPSite cmdlet enables you to easily move a site collection from one content database to another. All that is needed to execute this cmdlet is the site collection identity and the destination database name. Listing 8.17 shows a sample command line.

LISTING 8.17 **Moving a Site Collection to a Different Content Database**

```
Move-SPSite -Identity "http://sp2013/sites/sitecol"
-DestinationDatabase "WSS_CONTENT_TEAMSITES"
```

You do not need to provide the originating database because no parameter exists for that anyway. The destination database must already exist.

Move All Site Collections from One Content Database to Another

Scenario/Problem: You want to move all site collections stored in one content database to a different content database.

Solution: Use the `Move-SPSite` cmdlet with the `Get-SPSite` cmdlet.

You can pipe the results of `Get-SPSite` to the `Move-SPSite` cmdlet. Therefore, by using the `ContentDatabase` parameter with `Get-SPSite`, you can easily move all site collections from that content database to a new content database. Listing 8.18 shows a sample command line.

LISTING 8.18 **Moving All Site Collections from a Content Database**

```
Get-SPSite -ContentDatabase "WSS_CONTENT_MAIN" | Move-SPSite
-DestinationDatabase "WSS_CONTENT_TEAMSITES"
```

As with moving a single site collection, the destination database must already exist.

TIP Use the `New-SPContentDatabase` cmdlet to quickly generate a new content database to move your site collection.

Display All Deleted Site Collections

Scenario/Problem: You need to obtain a deleted site collection reference and therefore need a listing of deleted site collections regardless of content database.

Solution: Use the `Get-SPDeletedSite` cmdlet without any parameters.

To obtain a deleted site collection reference object, you need to find the URL (`Identity`) or Site Id of the site collection. Using the `Get-SPDeletedSite` cmdlet displays all deleted site collections, as shown in Figure 8.2.

FIGURE 8.2 The `Get-SPDeletedSite` cmdlet displays all deleted sites.

Display Deleted Site Collections in a Content Database

Scenario/Problem: You need to obtain a site collection reference and therefore need a listing of available site collection URLs within a specific content database.

Solution: Use the `Get-SPDeletedSite` cmdlet with the `ContentDatabase` parameter.

To obtain a deleted site collection reference object, you need to find the Path or Site Id of the site collection. Using the `Get-SPDeletedSite` cmdlet with the `ContentDatabase` parameter, as shown in Listing 8.19, displays all deleted site collections in the specified content database.

LISTING 8.19 **Displaying Deleted Site Collections in a Content Database**

```
Get-SPDeletedSite -ContentDatabase "WSS_CONTENT"
```

TIP Use the `New-SPContentDatabase` cmdlet to quickly generate a new content database to move your site collections.

Get a Specific Deleted Site Collection

Scenario/Problem: You need to obtain a specific deleted site collection reference.

Solution: Use the `Get-SPDeletedSite` cmdlet to assign a variable the results using the `-Identity` parameter.

Providing the identity of the deleted site collection with the `Get-SPDeletedSite` cmdlet retrieves a specific site collection. Use this to assign the results to an object for use in other cmdlets, as shown in Listing 8.20.

LISTING 8.20 **Assigning a Variable to a Specific Deleted Site Collection**

```
$deletedSiteCol = Get-SPDeletedSite -Identity " /sites/deletedsitecol"
```

The `Identity` parameter, in this case, is the path shown when retrieving all site collections (`Get-SPDeletedSite`).

Remove a Deleted Site Collection

Scenario/Problem: You need to remove a deleted site collection from your SharePoint farm.

Solution: Use the `Remove-SPDeletedSite` cmdlet with a site collection variable.

The `Remove-SPDeletedSite` cmdlet enables you to remove a specific site collection from the current server. Use this in conjunction with the `Get-SPDeletedSite` cmdlet (explained in a previous section), as shown in Listing 8.21, or just use the site collection identity directly in line, as shown in Listing 8.22.

LISTING 8.21 **Removing a Site Collection Using a Variable**

```
$deletedSiteCol = Get-SPDeletedSite -Identity "/ sites/ deletedsitecol "
Remove-SPDeletedSite $deletedSiteCol
```

LISTING 8.22 **Removing a Deleted Site Collection Directly**

```
Remove-SPDeletedSite -Identity " /sites/deletedsitecol"
```

Restore a Deleted Site Collection

Scenario/Problem: You need to restore a previously deleted site collection on your SharePoint farm.

Solution: Use the `Restore-SPDeletedSite` cmdlet with a deleted site collection variable.

The `Restore-SPDeletedSite` cmdlet enables you to restore a deleted site collection from the current farm. Use this in conjunction with the `Get-SPDeletedSite` cmdlet (explained in a previous section), as shown in Listing 8.23, or just use the site collection identity directly in line, as shown in Listing 8.24.

LISTING 8.23 **Restoring a Deleted Site Collection Using a Variable**

```
$deletedSiteCol = Get-SPDeletedSite -Identity "/ sites/deletedsitecol"
Restore-SPDeletedSite $deletedSiteCol
```

LISTING 8.24 **Restoring a Deleted Site Collection Directly**

```
Restore-SPDeletedSite -Identity " /sites/deletedsitecol"
```

Configure Information Rights Management (IRM) Settings

Scenario/Problem: You want to script out Information Rights Management settings.

Solution: Use the cmdlets listed in this section to configure IRM settings.

This chapter covers the basic or more common site management cmdlets. SharePoint 2013 provides advance scripting for IRM settings. As such, the following cmdlets nouns are now available:

▶ `SPIRMSettings`

▶ `SPSiteSubscriptionIRMConfig`

CHAPTER 9

Solutions and Features

This chapter outlines the SharePoint PowerShell commands used to manage the solutions and features throughout the SharePoint farm and sites. Solutions are installed on the farm and deployed to specific site collections or globally. Solutions can contain features that become available at the site or site collection levels. Using the cmdlets in this chapter assists in automating the management of these solutions and features.

Add a Solution to the SharePoint Farm

Scenario/Problem: You need to add a solution to the farm using a script.

Solution: Use the `Add-SPSolution` cmdlet.

Using the `Add-SPSolution` cmdlet adds a solution package (.wsp) to the farm. All you need to provide the cmdlet is the actual location of the solution package, as shown in Listing 9.1.

LISTING 9.1 **Adding a Solution to the SharePoint Farm**

```
Add-SPSolution "c:\newsolution.wsp"
```

The solution location is the `-LiteralPath` parameter, which is required. The path can be a local drive location or network location using a UNC string (`\\servername\folder`).

Display Available Solutions on the Farm

Scenario/Problem: You need to obtain a solution reference and therefore need a listing of available solutions.

Solution: Use the `Get-SPSolution` cmdlet without any parameters to retrieve all available solutions.

To obtain a solution reference object, you need to find the identity of the solution. Using the `Get-SPSolution` cmdlet by itself (see Listing 9.2) displays all available solutions deployed to the current farm.

LISTING 9.2 **Displaying All Available Solutions**

```
Get-SPSolution
```

Get a Specific Solution

Scenario/Problem: You need to obtain a specific solution reference.

Solution: Use the `Get-SPSolution` cmdlet to assign a variable the results using the `-Identity` parameter.

Providing the identity of the solution with the `Get-SPSolution` cmdlet retrieves a specific solution. Use this to assign the results to an object for use in other cmdlets, as shown in Listing 9.3.

LISTING 9.3 **Assigning a Variable to a Specific Solution**

```
$solution = Get-SPSolution
-Identity c0e31dec-294d-4f2d-9ae4-f2e637c766bd
```

TIP Instead of using the solution GUID, you may instead use the name of the solution as listed in the output when issuing `Get-SPSolution` without any parameters.

Deploy a Solution to a Web Application

Scenario/Problem: You need to deploy a solution that was added to the farm to a web application.

Solution: Use the `Install-SPSolution` cmdlet with a solution variable.

The `Install-SPSolution` cmdlet enables you to deploy a specific solution installed on the farm to a specified web application. Use this in conjunction with the `Get-SPSolution` cmdlet (explained in a previous section), as shown in Listing 9.4.

LISTING 9.4 **Sample Configuration Script for Deploying a Solution**

```
$solution = Get-SPSolution
-Identity c0e31dec-294d-4f2d-9ae4-f2e637c766bd
Install-SPSolution $solution -WebApplication "SharePoint - 80"
-Force -GACDeployment
```

NOTE You may only deploy a solution to a web application if the solution contains components that are scoped at the web application level. To install globally, do not include the `-WebApplication` parameter.

The `-Force` switch parameter forces the solution to be deployed to the specified web application. As noted, if no components are scoped for the web application level, you cannot force the solution to be deployed to the web application. However, if you are deploying the solution globally, the `-Force` parameter redeploys the solution if it has already been previously deployed.

The `-GACDeployment` switch parameter needs to be included if assemblies in the solution will be deployed to the Global Assembly Cache (GAC). Most of the time, this is the case—especially with third-party products.

If code access security (CAS) policies are included in the solution, you need to provide the `-CASPolicies` switch parameter to the `Install-SPSolution` command. This is less common but does occur.

> **TIP** To deploy to all web applications, instead of providing a specific web application (using the `-WebApplication` parameter), use the `-AllWebApplications` switch parameter.

Retract a Solution

> **Scenario/Problem:** You need to retract a deployed solution from a web application or global deployment.

Solution: Use the `UnInstall-SPSolution` cmdlet with a solution variable.

The `Uninstall-SPSolution` cmdlet enables you to retract a specific solution that was previously deployed. Use this in conjunction with the `Get-SPSolution` cmdlet (explained in a previous section), as shown in Listing 9.5.

LISTING 9.5 **Retracting a Solution from a Web Application**

```
$solution = Get-SPSolution
-Identity c0e31dec-294d-4f2d-9ae4-f2e637c766bd
Uninstall-SPSolution $solution -WebApplication "SharePoint - 80"
```

Providing the `-WebApplication` parameter retracts the solution from the specified web application (assuming that the solution was deployed to that web application and has resources scoped at the web application level). You also can retract the solution from all web applications, as shown in Listing 9.6.

LISTING 9.6 **Retracting a Solution from All Web Applications**

```
$solution = Get-SPSolution
-Identity c0e31dec-294d-4f2d-9ae4-f2e637c766bd
Uninstall-SPSolution $solution -AllWebApplications
```

If the solution is installed globally, all you need to provide to the Uninstall-SPSolution cmdlet is the solution identity, as shown in Listing 9.7.

LISTING 9.7 **Retracting a Solution That Was Globally Deployed**

```
$solution = Get-SPSolution
-Identity c0e31dec-294d-4f2d-9ae4-f2e637c766bd
Uninstall-SPSolution $solution
```

Upgrade a Deployed Solution

Scenario/Problem: You have an updated solution package that needs to be deployed to SharePoint.

Solution: Use the Update-SPSolution cmdlet with a solution variable.

The Update-SPSolution cmdlet enables you to upgrade a previously deployed solution with a newer version of the solution package (and underlying files). Use this in conjunction with the Get-SPSolution cmdlet (explained in a previous section), as shown in Listing 9.8.

LISTING 9.8 **Sample Configuration Script for Upgrading a Solution**

```
$solution = Get-SPSolution
-Identity c0e31dec-294d-4f2d-9ae4-f2e637c766bd
Update-SPSolution $solution -LiteralPath "c:\newsolution.wsp" -Force
-GACDeployment
```

The -LiteralPath determines the location of the updated solution package. The path can be a local drive location or network location using a UNC string (\\servername\folder).

The -Force switch parameter forces the solution to be upgraded.

The -GACDeployment switch parameter needs to be included if assemblies in the solution will be redeployed to the Global Assembly Cache (GAC).

If code access security (CAS) policies are included in the solution, you need to provide the -CASPolicies switch parameter to the Update-SPSolution command.

NOTE If there are new files or changes to the underlying structure, you may not be able to upgrade the existing solution. In this case, you need to retract and remove the solution from the farm and then add the updated package as a new solution.

Remove a Solution from the SharePoint Farm

Scenario/Problem: You need to remove a solution from the SharePoint farm.

Solution: Use the `Remove-SPSolution` cmdlet with a solution variable.

The `Remove-SPSolution` cmdlet enables you to remove a specific solution from the current farm. Use this in conjunction with the `Get-SPSolution` cmdlet (explained in a previous section), as shown in Listing 9.9.

LISTING 9.9 **Sample Configuration Script for Removing a Solution**

```
$solution = Get-SPSolution
-Identity c0e31dec-294d-4f2d-9ae4-f2e637c766bd
Remove-SPSolution $solution
```

NOTE You may not remove a solution that has been deployed. You must first retract the solution and then perform the removal operation.

Add a Sandboxed Solution to a Site Collection

Scenario/Problem: You need to add a sandboxed solution to a specific site collection.

Solution: Use the `Add-SPUserSolution` cmdlet.

Using the `Add-SPUserSolution` cmdlet adds a solution package (.wsp) to a site collection. All you need to provide the cmdlet is the actual location of the sandboxed solution package and the site collection, as shown in Listing 9.10.

LISTING 9.10 **Adding a Sandboxed Solution to a Site Collection**

```
Add-SPUserSolution -LiteralPath "c:\SBSolution.wsp" -Site
"http://intranet.sp2013.com/sites/UserSC"
```

The sandboxed solution package location is the `-LiteralPath` parameter, which is required. The path can be a local drive location or network location using a UNC string (`\\servername\folder`).

The `-Site` parameter is the site collection path to which the sandboxed solution should be deployed.

Display Available Sandboxed Solutions in a Site Collection

Scenario/Problem: You need to obtain a sandboxed solution reference and therefore need a listing of available solutions.

Solution: Use the Get-SPUserSolution cmdlet with a specified site collection.

To obtain a sandboxed solution reference object, you need to find the identity of the sandboxed solution. Using Get-SPUserSolution with the -Site parameter displays all available sandboxed solutions, as shown in Listing 9.11.

LISTING 9.11 **Displaying All Available Sandboxed Solutions**

```
Get-SPUserSolution -site "http://intranet.sp2013.com/sites/UserSC"
```

Get a Specific Sandboxed Solution

Scenario/Problem: You need to obtain a specific solution reference.

Solution: Use the Get-SPUserSolution cmdlet to assign a variable the results using the -Identity parameter.

Providing the identity of the sandboxed solution with the Get-SPUserSolution cmdlet retrieves a specific sandboxed solution. Use this to assign the results to an object for use in other cmdlets, as shown in Listing 9.12.

LISTING 9.12 **Assigning a Variable to a Specific Sandboxed Solution**

```
$userSolution = Get-SPUserSolution
-Identity c0e31dec-294d-4f2d-9ae4-f2e637c766bd
-site "http://intranet.sp2013.com/sites/UserSC"
```

TIP Instead of using the solution GUID, you may use the name of the solution as listed in the output when issuing Get-SPUserSolution.

Activate a Sandboxed Solution

Scenario/Problem: You need to activate a sandboxed solution that was added to the site collection.

Solution: Use the `Install-SPUserSolution` cmdlet with a sandboxed solution variable and site collection reference.

The `Install-SPUserSolution` cmdlet enables you to deploy a specific sandboxed solution installed on the farm to a specified web application. Use this in conjunction with the `Get-SPUserSolution` cmdlet (explained in a previous section), as shown in Listing 9.13.

LISTING 9.13 **Sample Configuration Script for Deploying a Sandboxed Solution**

```
$userSolution = Get-SPUserSolution
-Identity c0e31dec-294d-4f2d-9ae4-f2e637c766bd
Install-SPUserSolution $userSolution -Site "http://intranet.sp2013.com/
➥sites/UserSC"
```

Deactivate a Sandboxed Solution

> **Scenario/Problem:** You need to deactivate an active sandboxed solution from a site collection.

Solution: Use the `UnInstall-SPUserSolution` cmdlet with a sandboxed solution variable and site collection reference.

The `Uninstall-SPUserSolution` cmdlet enables you to deactivate a specific sandboxed solution that was previously deployed. Use this in conjunction with the `Get-SPUserSolution` cmdlet (explained in a previous section), as shown in Listing 9.14.

LISTING 9.14 **Retracting a Sandboxed Solution from a Site Collection**

```
$userSolution = Get-SPUserSolution
-Identity c0e31dec-294d-4f2d-9ae4-f2e637c766bd
Uninstall-SPUserSolution $userSolution -Site "http://intranet.sp2013.com/
➥sites/UserSC"
```

Upgrade a Deployed Sandboxed Solution

> **Scenario/Problem:** You have an updated sandboxed solution package that needs to be deployed to a site collection.

Solution: Use the `Update-SPUserSolution` cmdlet with a sandboxed solution variable.

The Update-SPUserSolution cmdlet enables you to upgrade a previously deployed sandboxed solution with a newer version of the sandboxed solution package (and underlying files). You first need to add the new package to the site collection, as shown in Listing 9.15.

LISTING 9.15 **Sample Configuration Script for Upgrading a Sandboxed Solution**

```
Add-SPUserSolution -LiteralPath "c:\SBSolution2.wsp"
-Site "http://intranet.sp2013.com/sites/UserSC"
$userSolution = Get-SPUserSolution
-Identity c0e31dec-294d-4f2d-9ae4-f2e637c766bd
Update-SPUserSolution $userSolution
-site "http://intranet.sp2013.com/sites/UserSC"
-ToSolution SBSolution2
```

Remove a Sandboxed Solution from a Site Collection

Scenario/Problem: You need to remove a sandboxed solution from a site collection.

Solution: Use the Remove-SPUserSolution cmdlet with a sandboxed solution variable.

The Remove-SPUserSolution cmdlet enables you to remove a specific sandboxed solution from a specified site collection. Use this in conjunction with the Get-SPUserSolution cmdlet (explained in a previous section), as shown in Listing 9.16.

LISTING 9.16 **Sample Configuration Script for Removing a Sandboxed Solution**

```
$userSolution = Get-SPUserSolution
-Identity c0e31dec-294d-4f2d-9ae4-f2e637c766bd
Remove-SPUserSolution $userSolution
-site "http://intranet.sp2013.com/sites/UserSC"
```

NOTE You may not remove a solution that has been deployed. You must first retract the solution and then perform the removal operation.

Display Available Features

Scenario/Problem: You need to obtain a feature reference and therefore need a listing of available features.

Solution: Use the `Get-SPFeature` cmdlet using the desired scope.

The `Get-SPFeature` cmdlet is handy for listing the installed features at various levels within your SharePoint environment. Issuing the command without any parameters displays all features at every level. Because there are about 12 dozen features at all levels, listing them all is usually not helpful.

Luckily, the `Get-SPFeature` cmdlet has several parameter sets you can use to narrow your list of features. To display the features at the farm level, simply use the `-Farm` switch parameter, as shown in Listing 9.17.

LISTING 9.17 **Displaying All Installed Farm Features**

```
Get-SPFeature -Farm
```

To display the features at the web application level, use the `-WebApplication` parameter and provide the web application name or identity, as shown in Listing 9.18.

LISTING 9.18 **Displaying All Installed Web Application Features**

```
Get-SPFeature -WebApplication "SharePoint - 80"
```

This also works for site collection and site features. For site collections, use the `-Site` parameter (see Listing 9.19); for site features, use the `-Web` parameter (see Listing 9.20).

LISTING 9.19 **Displaying All Installed Site Collection Features**

```
Get-SPFeature -Site "http://sp2013"
```

LISTING 9.20 **Displaying All Installed Site Features**

```
Get-SPFeature -Web "http://sp2013"
```

Get a Specific Feature

Scenario/Problem: You need to obtain a specific feature reference.

Solution: Use the `Get-SPFeature` cmdlet to assign a variable to the results using the `-Identity` parameter.

Providing the identity of the solution with the `Get-SPSolution` cmdlet retrieves a specific solution. Use this to assign the results to an object for use in other cmdlets, as shown in Listing 9.21.

LISTING 9.21 **Assigning a Variable to a Specific Feature**

```
$feature = Get-SPFeature
-Identity e8389ec7-70fd-4179-a1c4-6fcb4342d7a0
```

TIP Although you may also retrieve the feature using its display name, it is recommended to use the feature GUID such that the exact feature and scope can be determined. The feature GUID uniquely identifies the feature, whereas there could be a site collection and site -level feature using the same display name.

Activate a Feature

Scenario/Problem: You need to activate a feature.

Solution: Use the Enable-SPFeature cmdlet with a feature variable.

The Enable-SPFeature cmdlet enables you to activate a feature at the determined level. Use this in conjunction with the Get-SPFeature cmdlet (explained in the previous section), as shown in Listing 9.22.

LISTING 9.22 **Sample Script for Activating a Feature**

```
$feature = Get-SPFeature
-Identity e8389ec7-70fd-4179-a1c4-6fcb4342d7a0
Enable-SPFeature $feature -Url "http://sp2013" -Force
```

The -Url parameter is either the web application, site collection, or the site in which the feature should be activated. At the root level of the main site, the address is the same. Features can be activated only at the level where they reside.

The -Force switch parameter forces the activation and reruns any customized code. This occurs if the feature is already activated and you are forcing a reactivation.

NOTE To enable farm features, do not provide a –Url parameter.

Deactivate a Feature

Scenario/Problem: You need to deactivate a feature.

Solution: Use the Disable-SPFeature cmdlet with a feature variable.

The `Disable-SPFeature` cmdlet enables you to deactivate a feature at the determined level. Use this in conjunction with the `Get-SPFeature` cmdlet (explained in a previous section), as shown in Listing 9.23.

LISTING 9.23 **Sample Script for Deactivating a Feature**

```
$feature = Get-SPFeature
-Identity e8389ec7-70fd-4179-a1c4-6fcb4342d7a0
Disable-SPFeature $feature -Url "http://sp2013" -Force
```

The `-Url` parameter is either the web application, site collection, or the site in which the feature should be activated. At the root level of the main site, the address is the same. Features can be deactivated only at the level where they reside and are activated.

The `-Force` switch parameter forces the deactivation and does not produce any errors if the feature is already deactivated.

NOTE To disable farm features, do not provide a `-Url` parameter.

Install a Feature in SharePoint

Scenario/Problem: You need to install a feature to SharePoint.

Solution: Use the `Install-SPFeature` cmdlet with the `-Path` parameter.

The `Install-SPFeature` cmdlet enables you to install a feature that already has been copied or deployed to the SharePoint environment. The feature files should reside within a folder under the `14\TEMPLATE\FEATURES` location of the SharePoint servers. The folder that contains the feature files is used as the `-Path` parameter with the `Install-SPFeature` cmdlet, as shown in Listing 9.24.

LISTING 9.24 **Sample Script for Installing a Feature**

```
Install-SPFeature -Path "CustomFeature" -Force
```

The `-Force` switch parameter forces the installation and does not produce any errors if the feature has already been installed.

NOTE The feature scope is contained within the feature.xml file and therefore no other parameters are required to perform the installation. The feature is available at the level of its scope.

Uninstall a Feature from SharePoint

Scenario/Problem: You need to uninstall a feature from SharePoint.

Solution: Use the `Uninstall-SPFeature` cmdlet with a feature variable.

The `Uninstall-SPFeature` cmdlet enables you to uninstall a feature from SharePoint. Use this in conjunction with the `Get-SPFeature` cmdlet (explained in a previous section), as shown in Listing 9.25.

LISTING 9.25 **Sample Script for Uninstalling a Feature**

```
$feature = Get-SPFeature
-Identity e8389ec7-70fd-4179-a1c4-6fcb4342d7a0
Uninstall-SPFeature $feature  -Force
```

The `-Force` switch parameter forces the feature to be uninstalled and does not produce any errors if the feature has already been uninstalled.

NOTE The feature scope is contained within the feature.xml file and therefore no other parameters are required to perform the uninstallation. The feature is uninstalled at the level of its scope. This does not remove the files in the feature folder, however.

Export Installed Farm Solutions

Scenario/Problem: You want to export the installed farm solutions to local files.

Solution: Create a script that loops through the solutions and saves them locally.

Using the SharePoint assemblies, you can easily generate a script that loops through the installed farm solutions and actually extracts them into their `.wsp` files on a local drive. This becomes extremely valuable when you are moving solutions from one environment to another (for example, from development to staging). Listing 9.26 shows a sample script.

LISTING 9.26 **Sample Script for Exporting All Farm Solutions**

```
[Void][System.Reflection.Assembly]::LoadWithPartialName(
"Microsoft.SharePoint")
[Void][System.Reflection.Assembly]::LoadWithPartialName(
```

```
"Microsoft.SharePoint.Administration")

    $spFarm = [Microsoft.SharePoint.Administration.SPFarm]::Local
    $spFarmSolutions = $spFarm.Solutions
    $localPath = "C:\Solutions\"

    foreach($spFarmSolution in $spFarmSolutions)
    {
        [string]$outputFileName = $localPath + $spFarmSolution.Name
        $spFarmSolution.SolutionFile.SaveAs($outputFileName);
    }
```

Set the $localPath variable to a location where you want the solution files to be extracted and saved.

CHAPTER 10

Content Deployment

This chapter explains how to use the SharePoint cmdlets to manage and administer content deployment within your SharePoint farm. Content deployment involves publishing internal content to another site (usually public facing). Your farm topology must be properly configured to implement content publishing and deployment.

Create a New Deployment Path

Scenario/Problem: You need to setup and configure a new deployment path.

Solution: Use the `New-SPContentDeploymentPath` cmdlet.

Setting up a new deployment path involves mapping the source web application and site to a target web application and site. You can use the `New-SPContentDeploymentPath` cmdlet to facilitate this mapping, as shown in Listing 10.1

LISTING 10.1 **Creating a New Content Deployment Path**

```
New-SPContentDeploymentPath -Name "Marketing Internet Content" -
SourceSPWebApplication "SharePoint - 80" -SourceSPSite
"http://intranet.sp2013.com/Marketing" -
DestinationCentralAdministrationURL "http://internet.sp2013.com:12345"
-DestinationSPWebApplication "SharePoint - Internet" -
DestinationSPSite "http://internet.sp2013.com/Marketing" -PathAccount
(Get-Credential)
```

TIP Use inline credentials instead of (Get-Credential). See Chapter 2, "PowerShell Basics," for more details.

The `-PathAccount` is used to authenticate to the destination server and site. Therefore, this account must have the appropriate permissions and should be an administrator of the destination Central Administration.

NOTE The destination Central Administration server must be configured to accept content deployment jobs before the path can be created.

Display Deployment Paths Configured on the Farm

Scenario/Problem: You need to identify deployment paths for proper job creation.

Solution: Use the `Get-SPContentDeploymentPath` cmdlet without any parameters to retrieve all available content deployment paths.

To obtain a content deployment path reference object, you need to find the identity of the path entry. Use the `Get-SPContentDeploymentPath` by itself, as shown in Listing 10.2, to display all available content deployment paths.

LISTING 10.2 **Display All Available Content Deployment Paths**

```
Get-SPContentDeploymentPath
```

Get a Specific Content Deployment Path

> **Scenario/Problem:** You need to obtain a specific content deployment path reference.

Solution: Use the `Get-SPContentDeploymentPath` cmdlet to assign a variable the results using the `-Identity` parameter.

Providing the identity of the content deployment path with the `Get-SPContent DeploymentPath` cmdlet retrieves a specific content deployment path. Use this to assign the results to an object for use in other cmdlets, as shown in Listing 10.3.

LISTING 10.3 **Assigning a Variable to a Specific Content Deployment Path**

```
$path = Get-SPContentDeploymentPath -Identity "Marketing Internet
Content"
```

Remove a Content Deployment Path

> **Scenario/Problem:** You need to delete a content deployment path configuration from the SharePoint farm.

Solution: Use the `Remove-SPContentDeploymentPath` cmdlet.

The `Remove-SPContentDeploymentPath` cmdlet enables you to remove a specific content deployment path configured on the current farm. Simply provide the name of the content deployment path, as shown in Listing 10.4.

LISTING 10.4 **Remove a Specific Content Deployment Path**

```
Remove-SPContentDeploymentPath "Marketing Internet Content"
```

> **NOTE** You may not remove a path that has a content deployment job configured. Remove the deployment job first before removing the deployment path.

Create a New Deployment Job

> **Scenario/Problem:** You need to setup and configure a new deployment job.

Solution: Use the `New-SPContentDeploymentJob` cmdlet.

Setting up a new deployment job involves mapping the source web application and site to a target web application and site. You can use the `New-SPContentDeploymentJob` cmdlet to facilitate this mapping, as shown in Listing 10.5

LISTING 10.5 **Creating a New Content Deployment Job**

```
New-SPContentDeploymentJob -Name "Marketing Deployment Job" -
SPContentDeploymentPath "Marketing Internet Content"
```

The `-SPContentDeploymentPath` is the name of the deployment path used for this deployment job.

> **NOTE** A content deployment path must be configured first before a content deployment job can be created.

Display Deployment Jobs Configured on the Farm

> **Scenario/Problem:** You need to identify deployment paths for proper job creation.

Solution: Use the `Get-SPContentDeploymentJob` cmdlet without any parameters to retrieve all available deployment jobs.

To obtain a content deployment job reference object, you need to find the identity of the job entry. Using the `Get-SPContentDeploymentJob` by itself, as shown in Listing 10.6, displays all deployment jobs.

LISTING 10.6 **Display All Available Content Deployment Jobs**

```
Get-SPContentDeploymentJob
```

Get a Specific Content Deployment Job

Scenario/Problem: You need to obtain a specific content deployment path reference.

Solution: Use the `Get-SPContentDeploymentJob` cmdlet to assign a variable the results using the `-Identity` parameter.

Providing the identity of the content deployment job with the `Get-SPContentDeploymentJob` cmdlet retrieves a specific content deployment job. Use this to assign the results to an object for use in other cmdlets, as shown in Listing 10.7.

LISTING 10.7 **Assigning a Variable to a Specific Content Deployment Job**

```
$job = Get-SPContentDeploymentJob -Identity "Marketing Deployment Job"
```

Remove a Content Deployment Job

Scenario/Problem: You need to delete a content deployment path configuration from the SharePoint farm.

Solution: Use the `Remove-SPContentDeploymentJob` cmdlet.

The `Remove-SPContentDeploymentJob` cmdlet enables you to remove a specific deployment job from the current farm. Simply provide the name of the content deployment job, as shown in Listing 10.8.

LISTING 10.8 **Remove a Specific Content Deployment Job**

```
Remove-SPContentDeploymentJob "Marketing Deployment Job"
```

Start a Content Deployment Job

Scenario/Problem: You need to kick off a deployment job such that content is deployed from the source site to the target site.

Solution: Use the `Start-SPContentDeploymentJob` cmdlet.

The `Start-SPContentDeploymentJob` cmdlet enables you to manually start a content deployment job. Simply provide the name of the content deployment job, as shown in Listing 10.9.

LISTING 10.9 **Manually Start a Specific Content Deployment Job**

```
Start-SPContentDeploymentJob "Marketing Deployment Job"
```

Modify Content Deployment Configurations

Scenario/Problem: You need to modify properties of content deployment paths or jobs

Solution: Use the cmdlets listed in this section to change the configuration of existing deployment paths and jobs.

This chapter covers the basic or more common cmdlets for managing content deployments. For more advance scripting and modifications of content deployment jobs and paths, the following cmdlets are available:

- `Set-SPContentDeploymentPath`
- `Set-SPContentDeploymentJob`

CHAPTER 11

User Licensing

This chapter outlines the SharePoint PowerShell commands used to manage user licenses in SharePoint 2013. Previous versions of SharePoint had no mechanism to match user licenses with the SharePoint server licenses. Therefore, users with standard licenses, for example, could still access SharePoint Enterprise features. Using the new SharePoint PowerShell User License cmdlets enables you to enforce user licensing and create appropriate license mappings against security groups.

Display User Licensing Status

Scenario/Problem: You need to determine if licensing is being enforced.

Solution: Use the `Get-SPUserLicensing` cmdlet without any parameters to retrieve the status.

To display the user licensing status, simply use the `Get-SPUserLicensing` by itself as shown in Listing 11.1.

LISTING 11.1 **Displaying the Status of User Licensing Enforcement**

```
Get-SPUserLicensing
```

The `Get-SPUserLicensing` cmdlet displays the current status of user license enforcement and returns an `Enabled` property, as shown in Figure 11.1.

FIGURE 11.1 The `Get-SPUserLicensing` cmdlet displays the current status.

Enable User Licensing Enforcement

Scenario/Problem: You would like to enable user licensing enforcement.

Solution: Use the `Enable-SPUserLicensing` cmdlet without any parameters to enable user licensing.

By default, user licensing enforcement is disabled. Using the `Enable-SPUserLicensing` cmdlet without any parameters, as shown in Listing 11.2, enables the user licensing enforcement within the current SharePoint farm. Use the `Get-SPUserLicensing` cmdlet, as explained in the previous section, to verify enablement.

LISTING 11.2 **Enabling the Status of User Licensing Enforcement**

```
Enable-SPUserLicensing
```

Disable User Licensing Enforcement

Scenario/Problem: You would like to disable user licensing enforcement.

Solution: Use the `Disable-SPUserLicensing` cmdlet without any parameters to disable user licensing.

Using the `Disable-SPUserLicensing` cmdlet without any parameters, as shown in Listing 11.3, disables the user licensing enforcement within the current SharePoint farm. Use the `Get-SPUserLicensing` cmdlet, as explained in the previous section, to verify disablement.

LISTING 11.3 **Disabling User Licensing Enforcement**

```
Disable-SPUserLicensing
```

Display Available User Licenses

Scenario/Problem: You need to determine which licenses are available for mapping purposes.

Solution: Use the `Get-SPUserLicense` cmdlet without any parameters to retrieve the available user license types.

LISTING 11.4 **Displaying the Available User Licenses**

```
Get-SPUserLicense
```

The `Get-SPUserLicense` cmdlet displays the available user licenses, as shown in Figure 11.2.

FIGURE 11.2 The Get-SPUserLicensing cmdlet displays the available licenses.

Create a New License Mapping

Scenario/Problem: You need to create a new license mapping to add to user licensing enforcement.

Solution: Use the New-SPUserLicenseMapping cmdlet with either the SecurityGroup, Role, ClaimType, or Claim parameters.

Before you can add a license mapping to user license enforcement, you need to create a new license mapping object. Use the New-SPUserLicenseMapping cmdlet to create a new variable object, as shown in Listing 11.5.

LISTING 11.5 **Creating a New License Mapping**

```
$licenseMapping = New-SPUserLicenseMapping -SecurityGroup "Enterprise
➥Admins" -License Enterprise
```

You can create a mapping against a security group, a forms-based role, a claim type (with the original issuer specified), or a claim itself using the respective parameters. Reviewing the object displays the various properties of the mapping, as shown in Figure 11.3.

Add a New License Mapping

Scenario/Problem: You need to add a new license mapping to user license enforcement.

Solution: Use the Add-SPUserLicenseMapping cmdlet with the Mapping parameter.

FIGURE 11.3 Viewing a new license mapping object.

When a new license mapping object is created (as explained in the previous section), you can pass that object variable into the Add-SPUserLicenseMapping cmdlet using the -Mapping parameter, as shown in Listing 11.6.

LISTING 11.6 **Adding a New License Mapping**

```
$licenseMapping = New-SPUserLicenseMapping -SecurityGroup
"Enterprise Admins" -License Enterprise
Add-SPUserLicenseMapping -Mapping $licenseMapping
```

Display All License Mappings

Scenario/Problem: You need to review a list of added license mappings.

Solution: Use the Get-SPUserLicenseMapping cmdlet without any parameters.

You might need to see all license mappings that have been created or retrieve the identity of a specific license mapping. Use the Get-SPUserLicenseMapping cmdlet without any parameters, as shown in Listing 11.7, to retrieve a listing of all license mappings.

LISTING 11.7 **Displaying All License Mappings**

```
Get-SPUserLicenseMapping
```

Use the optional -WebApplication parameter to view only mappings associated with a particular web application.

Remove a License Mapping

Scenario/Problem: You need to remove a previously added license mapping.

Solution: Use the `Remove-SPUserLicenseMapping` cmdlet with the Identity parameter.

To remove a previously added license mapping, use the `Remove-SPUserLicenseMapping` cmdlet, providing the identity of the license mapping as shown in Listing 11.8.

LISTING 11.8 **Removing a License Mapping**

```
Remove-SPUserLicenseMapping -Identity 3bd51156-49fd-4122-85d0-
➡58f7019bf270
```

Use the `Get-SPUserLicenseMapping` cmdlet explained in the previous section to both retrieve the GUID identity of the license mapping you want to remove and, afterward, verify that the mapping was removed.

CHAPTER 12

InfoPath Forms Services

This chapter explores the administrative aspects of InfoPath Form Services through the use of PowerShell.

Browser-Enabled Form Templates

Scenario/Problem: You need to allow custom SharePoint forms to be rendered within SharePoint.

Solution: Use the `Set-SPInfoPathFormsService` cmdlet.

From the PowerShell cmdlet prompt, enter the following:

```
Set-SPInfoPathFormsService -AllowUserFormBrowserEnabling $true
-AllowUserFormBrowserRendering $true
```

TIP To disable the browser-enabled form templates, replace $true with $false.

Throttle Data Connection Timeouts

Scenario/Problem: You need to increase or decrease the data connection timeout limit.

Solution: Use the `Set-SPInfoPathFormsService` cmdlet with the data connection timeout parameters.

Your form attempts to connect and access data sources based on your configured data connections. If the data source is inaccessible, busy, or down, InfoPath Forms Services needs a way to time out the connection so that the form or the browser doesn't stop responding.

Use the `-DefaultDataConnectionTimeout` and `-MaxDataConnectionTimeout` parameters with the `Set-SPInfoPathFormsService` cmdlet to set the timeout values, as shown in Listing 12.1.

LISTING 12.1 **Data Connection Timeout Cmdlet Line**

```
Set-SPInfoPathFormsService -DefaultDataConnectionTimeout 15000
-MaxDataConnectionTimeout 25000
```

The timeout values are in milliseconds. The default value for `DefaultDataConnectionTimeout` is 10000 (10,000 milliseconds, or 10 seconds),

whereas the default value for `MaxDataConnectionTimeout` is `20000` (20,000 milliseconds, or 20 seconds).

> **TIP** The default values are usually acceptable entries and do not need to be modified. However, if you have some long-running data processes or connectivity issues, you may want to increase these numbers slightly.

Throttle the Data Connection Response Size

> **Scenario/Problem:** You need to increase or decrease the data connection response size.

Solution: Use the `MaxDataConnectionResponseSize` parameter with the `Set-SPInfoPathFormsService` cmdlet.

When connecting to data sources, you do not want to overload other systems. Limiting the response size determines how many kilobytes the data connection can process. You can modify the setting by using the `MaxDataConnectionReponseSize` parameter with the number of kilobytes, as shown in Listing 12.2.

LISTING 12.2 **Data Connection Response Size Cmdlet Line**

```
Set-SPInfoPathFormsService -MaxDataConnectionResponseSize 3000
```

> **TIP** The default value of 1500 (1,500KB) is usually a good setting. You do not want to strain other systems or databases. This also helps limit traffic on the network. Only increase this value if you have a large form that submits a great deal of data.

Modify Authentication Settings

> **Scenario/Problem:** You need to modify authentication settings.

Solution: Use the `Set-SPInfoPathFormsService` cmdlet with the appropriate parameters.

Several data authentication options either allow or prohibit certain types of data connectivity, as follows:

▶ **RequireSslForDataConnections:** Set this option to `true` to require SSL encryption when your form uses HTTP authentication (such as when accessing a web service).

▶ **AllowEmbeddedSqlForDataConnection:** Set this option to true if you have data connection files that contain SQL database connection information, including the username and password.

▶ **AllowUdcAuthenticationForDataConnections:** Set this option to true to allow custom forms to access data sources through data connection files.

▶ **AllowUserFormCrossDomainDataConnections:** Select this option if your form needs to access data sources on a different domain than SharePoint.

To configure these settings, use the Set-SPInfoPathFormsService cmdlet with the desired parameters and settings, as shown in Listing 12.3.

LISTING 12.3 **Authentication Settings Cmdlet Line**

```
Set-SPInfoPathFormsService -RequireSslForDataConnections $true
-AllowEmbeddedSqlForDataConnection $true
-AllowUdcAuthenticationForDataConnections $true
-AllowUserFormCrossDomainDataConnections $true
```

Configure Session State

Scenario/Problem: You want to configure session state settings.

Solution: Use the Set-SPInfoPathFormsService cmdlet with the appropriate parameters.

When a user is filling out a SharePoint form, InfoPath Form Services uses the SharePoint Server State service to manage user sessions. (You can switch this to View State using PowerShell; see the next section.) Transient data is stored within the session state.

Several settings are involved in the session state configuration:

▶ **MaxPostbacksPerSession:** Typically, not much chatter should take place between the form and Forms Services. This setting prevents unintended postbacks or "out-of-control" communications.

▶ **MaxUserActionsPerPostback:** Only a handful of actions should take place per postback. Again, this prevents a form process from pegging server resources.

▶ **ActiveSessionTimeout:** By default, active sessions are terminated after 1,440 minutes, which essentially is 24 hours. This is more of a cleanup process than anything. Some forms take a long time to fill out, depending on the information required, but one day should be plenty of time.

▶ **MaxSizeOfFormSessionState:** This determines how much data can be stored for the active user session. The default is 4,096KB, which equates to 4MB. This

provides plenty of room to store user session data. Typical forms and user information should take up only several kilobytes, at most.

If the user session lasts too long or too many postbacks to the server take place, the session is ended based on the configured settings. All form data is lost, and the user must start over. This is done to prevent unintended communication, limit network traffic, and limit system resource utilization.

To configure these settings, use the `Set-SPInfoPathFormsService` cmdlet with the desired parameters and settings, as shown in Listing 12.4.

LISTING 12.4 **Session State Settings Cmdlet Line**

```
Set-SPInfoPathFormsService -MaxPostbacksPerSession 110
-ActiveSessionTimeout 720
```

> **TIP** If forms are constantly being filled out within your organization and are fairly lightweight, you might actually want to reduce some of these values to keep recycling the session state as well as system resources. Another option is to use View State instead, as described in the next section.

Enable View State

> **Scenario/Problem:** Instead of using Session State, you would like to use View State.

Solution: Use the `AllowViewState` parameter with the `Set-SPInfoPathFormsService` cmdlet.

View state sessions (or Form View state) store session data within the client browser, thus reducing the load on the database server. Although this helps maximize database performance, more bandwidth is used in View state than in session state. The maximum session size allowed in View state is 40KB. If this limit is passed, the session automatically switches back to session state.

To configure these settings, use the `Set-SPInfoPathFormsService` cmdlet with the `-AllowViewState` and `-ViewStateThreshold` parameters, as shown in Listing 12.5.

LISTING 12.5 **View State Settings Cmdlet Line**

```
Set-SPInfoPathFormsService -AllowViewState $true -ViewStateThreshold
40961
```

> **TIP** You can only modify this setting using the PowerShell cmdlet line. There are no equivalent options in Central Administration.

Verify and Upload a Form Template

> **Scenario/Problem:** You need to verify and upload a form template to InfoPath Form Services.

Solution: Use the `Test-SPInfoPathFormTemplate` and `Install-SPInfoPathFormTemplate` PowerShell cmdlets to verify and upload the form template.

Forms that have code-behind or that require Full Trust permissions cannot be published directly to SharePoint. These forms must be published to a network location and then uploaded to Form Services. Before uploading, verify that the form is correct and can be installed.

To verify a form template, use the following cmdlet:

```
Test-SPInfoPathFormTemplate
-Path "<<full path to InfoPath form template>>"
```

To upload a form to InfoPath Form Services, use the following cmdlet:

```
Install-SPInfoPathFormTemplate
-Path "<<full path to InfoPath form template>>"
```

> **TIP** Use the switch parameter `-EnableGradualUpgrade` with `Install-SPInfoPathFormTemplate` to ensure that existing forms are upgraded.

Upload Multiple Form Templates at Once

> **Scenario/Problem:** You have many form templates to upload to InfoPath Form Services but find it difficult performing the same process for each one individually.

Solution: Pipe the paths of all form templates you want to upload to the `Install-SPInfoPathFormTemplate` cmdlet.

You can upload multiple form templates by listing out each path, separated by a comma, and then using the pipe (|) to pass that list into the `Install-SPInfoPathFormTemplate` cmdlet, as shown in Listing 12.6.

LISTING 12.6 **Multiple Form Upload Cmdlet Line**

```
"<<path of form 1>>" , "<<path of form 2>" , "<<path of form 3>>" |
Install-SPInfoPathFormTemplate
```

Activate or Deactivate a Form to or from a Site Collection

Scenario/Problem: You need to activate or deactivate a form to or from a site collection.

Solution: Use the `Enable-SPInfoPathFormTemplate` or `Disable-SPInfoPathFormTemplate` cmdlet.

When you upload a form, it generates and deploys a feature for your form to each site collection in your farm. Using the `Enable-SPInfoPathFormTemplate` cmdlet activates that feature on the site collection you choose. Conversely, using the `Disable-SPInfoPathFormTemplate` cmdlet deactivates the form feature of the selected site collection.

To activate a form to a site collection, use the following cmdlet:

```
Enable-SPInfoPathFormTemplate
-Identity "<<name of form template>>"
-Site "<<URL of Site Collection>>"
```

To deactivate a form from a site collection, use the following cmdlet:

```
Disable-SPInfoPathFormTemplate
-Identity "<<name of form template>>"
-Site "<<URL of Site Collection>>"
```

Remove a Form from InfoPath Form Services

Scenario/Problem: You need to remove a form from InfoPath Form Services.

Solution: Use the `Uninstall-SPInfoPathFormTemplate` PowerShell cmdlet.

Removing a form deletes it from InfoPath Forms Services. It is no longer available on any site collection. To remove a form from InfoPath Form Services, use the following cmdlet:

```
Uninstall-SPInfoPathFormTemplate -Identity "<<name of form template>>"
```

> **TIP** Removing a form does not always remove the content type it generates. Make sure the form is not being used anywhere in SharePoint. Otherwise, errors will occur when SharePoint tries to access the form template via the content type. (Hint: Remove the content type first because SharePoint will notify if it is being used.)

Quiesce a Form from InfoPath Form Services

Scenario/Problem: You need to quiesce a form from InfoPath Form Services.

Solution: Use the `Stop-SPInfoPathFormTemplate` PowerShell cmdlet.

Quiescing a form halts the initiation of new form instances and allows existing user sessions to complete. To quiesce a form from InfoPath Form Services, use the following cmdlet:

```
Stop-SPInfoPathFormTemplate -Identity "<<name of form template>>"
```

Enable the Web Service Proxy

Scenario/Problem: You need to enable the use of the InfoPath Form Services web service proxy.

Solution: Use the `Set-SPInfoPathWebServiceProxy` cmdlet.

The InfoPath Form Services web services proxy can be used to access web services without passing the credentials of the form user. A set of credentials for the web service needs to be stored within SharePoint's Secure Store Service (SSS), which is the replacement for Single Sign-On (SSO).

You need to modify a data connection file that your InfoPath form is using as a web service connection by adding a `UseFormsServiceProxy` attribute with a setting of `true` (see Listing 12.7), along with an `Authentication` element that references the Secure Store application ID (see Listing 12.8).

LISTING 12.7 **`UseFormsServiceProxy` Attribute in the Data Connection File**

```
<udc:ServiceUrl UseFormsServiceProxy="true"/>
```

LISTING 12.8 **Authentication Element in the Data Connection File**

```
<udc:Authentication>
    <udc:SSO AppId="<<AppID>>" CredentialType="<<credential type>>"/>
</udc:Authentication>
```

The possible credential types are as follows:

- Basic
- CD
- Digest
- Kerberos
- NTLM
- SQL

To enable the use of the web proxy, use the following cmdlet:

```
Set-SPInfoPathWebServiceProxy -Identity "<<URL of web application>>"
-AllowWebServiceProxy $true
```

To enable SharePoint forms to use the web proxy, use the following cmdlet:

```
Set-SPInfoPathWebServiceProxy -Identity "<<URL of web application>>"
-AllowForUserForms $true
```

> **TIP** The `AllowWebServiceProxy` setting needs to be set to `true` first before `AllowForUserForms` can be set to `true`. This is why the cmdlets need to be separated.

Export Forms Services Administration Files

> **Scenario/Problem:** You need to backup all of the form templates and data connection files that have been deployed to forms services.

Solution: Use the `Export-SPInfoPathAdministrationFiles` cmdlet.

You can use the `Export-SPInfoPathAdministrationFiles` cmdlet to produce a backup CAB file that contains all the forms and data connection files that have been deployed to the InfoPath Forms Services Application. Simply provide a path and filename, as shown in Listing 12.9. Optionally, you can provide the identity of the InfoPath Forms Service Application.

LISTING 12.9 **Backup InfoPath Forms Services Files to a CAB File**

```
Export -SPInfoPathAdministrationFiles -Path E:\IPBackup.CAB
```

Import Forms Services Administration Files

Scenario/Problem: You need to restore all of the form templates and data connection files that have been exported from forms services.

Solution: Use the `Import-SPInfoPathAdministrationFiles` cmdlet.

You can use the Import-SPInfoPathAdministrationFiles cmdlet to restore a backup CAB file to the InfoPath Forms Services Application. Simply provide the path and filename of the existing backup, as shown in Listing 12.10. Optionally, you can provide the identity of the InfoPath Forms Service Application.

LISTING 12.10 **Backup InfoPath Forms Services Files to a CAB File**

```
Import -SPInfoPathAdministrationFiles -Path E:\IPBackup.CAB
```

CHAPTER 13

Enterprise Search

This chapter explores the administrative aspects of Enterprise Search through the use of SharePoint PowerShell cmdlets.

Display the Enterprise Search Service Information

Scenario/Problem: You want to view the information on the Enterprise Search Service.

Solution: Use the `Get-SPEnterpriseSearchService` cmdlet.

The `Get-SPEnterpriseSearchService` cmdlet provides information on the Enterprise Search Service that is running on the SharePoint farm. No parameters are necessary, as shown in Listing 13.1.

LISTING 13.1 **Displaying the Enterprise Search Service Information**

```
Get-SPEnterpriseSearchService
```

The search service information is displayed, as shown in Figure 13.1.

FIGURE 13.1 Displaying the Enterprise Search Service information.

Display Enterprise Search Service Instances

Scenario/Problem: You want to view the information on the search service instances.

Solution: Use the `Get-SPEnterpriseSearchServiceInstance` cmdlet.

The Get-SPEnterpriseSearchServiceInstance cmdlet provides information on the Enterprise Search Service instances mapped to the search service. No parameters are necessary, as shown in Listing 13.2.

LISTING 13.2 **Displaying the Enterprise Search Service Instances**

```
Get-SPEnterpriseSearchServiceInstance
```

The Enterprise Search Service instance information is displayed, as shown in Figure 13.2.

FIGURE 13.2 Displaying the Enterprise Search Service instance information.

Get a Specific Enterprise Search Service Instance

Scenario/Problem: You need to obtain an Enterprise Search Service instance reference.

Solution: Use the Get-SPEnterpriseSearchServiceInstance cmdlet to assign a variable the results using the -Identity parameter.

Providing the identity of the Enterprise Search Service instance with the Get-SPEnterpriseSearchServiceInstance cmdlet retrieves a specific search service instance. Use this to assign the results to an object for use in other cmdlets, as shown in Listing 13.3.

LISTING 13.3 **Assigning a Variable to a Specific Search Service Application**

```
$ssInstance = Get-SPEnterpriseSearchServiceInstance
-Identity 91d00542-76cf-417b-aafb-dbfae76a1814
```

Configure the Crawl Account for Enterprise Search

> **Scenario/Problem:** You need to configure the crawl account for the Enterprise Search Service.

Solution: Use the `Set-SPEnterpriseSearchService` cmdlet with the crawl account parameters.

You may set the crawl account information for the search service by using the `ServiceAccount` and `ServicePassword` parameters with the `Set-SPEnterpriseSearchService` cmdlet, as shown in Listing 13.4.

LISTING 13.4 **Configuring the Search Service Crawl Account**

```
Set-SPEnterpriseSearchService
-Identity 9e19864d-8b4b-4fda-bcb1-10645457ad70
-ServiceAccount "SP\SharePointCrawl"
-ServicePassword (ConvertTo-SecureString -asplaintext -force
 -string "SharePoint1")
```

The password needs to be a secure string; therefore, the `ConvertTo-SecureString` cmdlet is used to assist. The Service Account setting is the Content Access Account when you are managing the Enterprise Search Service on the server.

Configure the Enterprise Search Service Performance Level

> **Scenario/Problem:** You need to change the performance level for the search service.

Solution: Use the `Set-SPEnterpriseSearchService` cmdlet with the `PerformanceLevel` parameter.

You can set the performance level using the `PerformanceLevel` parameter with the `Set-SPEnterpriseSearchService` cmdlet, as shown in Listing 13.5.

LISTING 13.5 **Configuring the Enterprise Search Service Performance Level**

```
Set-SPEnterpriseSearchService
-Identity 9e19864d-8b4b-4fda-bcb1-10645457ad70
-PerformanceLevel Reduced
```

The `PerformanceLevel` parameter determines how many threads the search service can use. The valid values are as follows:

▶ Reduced

▶ PartlyReduced

▶ Maximum

The default setting is `PartlyReduced`.

Display Enterprise Search Service Applications

Scenario/Problem: You want to view the information on the search service instances.

Solution: Use the `Get-SPEnterpriseSearchServiceApplication` cmdlet.

The `Get-SPEnterpriseSearchServiceApplication` cmdlet provides information on the Enterprise Search Service applications configured on the SharePoint farm. No parameters are necessary, as shown in Listing 13.6.

LISTING 13.6 **Displaying the Enterprise Search Service Applications**

```
Get-SPEnterpriseSearchServiceApplication
```

The Enterprise Search Service application information is displayed, as shown in Figure 13.3.

FIGURE 13.3 Displaying the Enterprise Search Service application information.

Get a Specific Enterprise Search Service Application

Scenario/Problem: You need to obtain an Enterprise Search Service application reference.

Solution: Use the `Get-SPEnterpriseSearchServiceApplication` cmdlet to assign a variable the results using the `-Identity` parameter.

Providing the identity of the Enterprise Search Service application with the `Get-SPEnterpriseSearchServiceApplication` cmdlet retrieves a specific Enterprise Search Service application. Use this to assign the results to an object for use in other cmdlets, as shown in Listing 13.7.

LISTING 13.7 **Assigning a Variable to a Specific Search Service Application**

```
$ssApp = Get-SPEnterpriseSearchServiceApplication
-Identity 81aedaf7-704c-47f4-8173-5e99a7495ac3
```

Create a Custom Metadata Category

Scenario/Problem: You want to create a metadata category for custom crawled properties.

Solution: Use the `New-SPEnterpriseSearchMetadataCategory` cmdlet.

Creating a metadata category enables you to organize your custom crawled properties. This makes managing custom search configurations easier. Creating a new category first enables you to use it when generating your crawled properties. You need to provide an Enterprise Search Service application reference, as shown in Listing 13.8.

LISTING 13.8 **Creating a New Metadata Category**

```
$ssApp = Get-SPEnterpriseSearchServiceApplication
-Identity 81aedaf7-704c-47f4-8173-5e99a7495ac3
New-SPEnterpriseSearchMetaDataCategory -Name "Custom Properties"
-SearchApplication $ssApp
```

You can use several switch parameter options when generating a new metadata category:

- ▶ `AutoCreateNewManagedProperties`
- ▶ `DiscoverNewProperties`
- ▶ `MapToContents`

Display Available Metadata Categories

Scenario/Problem: You want to view the information on the available search metadata categories.

Solution: Use the `Get-SPEnterpriseSearchMetadataCategory` cmdlet.

The `Get-SPEnterpriseSearchMetadataCategory` cmdlet provides information on the Enterprise Search metadata categories configured for a particular search service application. Therefore, you need to provide a search service application with this cmdlet, as shown in Listing 13.9.

LISTING 13.9 **Displaying the Search Metadata Categories**

```
$ssApp = Get-SPEnterpriseSearchServiceApplication
-Identity 81aedaf7-704c-47f4-8173-5e99a7495ac3
Get-SPEnterpriseSearchMetadataCategory -SearchApplication $ssApp
```

The Enterprise Search Service metadata categories are displayed, as shown in Figure 13.4.

FIGURE 13.4 Displaying the Enterprise Search Service application metadata categories.

Get a Specific Metadata Category

Scenario/Problem: You need to obtain a metadata category reference for use in other search cmdlets.

Solution: Use the `Get-SPEnterpriseSearchMetadataCategory` cmdlet to assign a variable the results using the `-Identity` and `-SearchApplication` parameters.

Providing the identity of the metadata category with the
Get-SPEnterpriseSearchMetadataCategory cmdlet retrieves a specific metadata
category for the specified search service application. Use this to assign the results to an
object for use in other cmdlets, as shown in Listing 13.10.

LISTING 13.10 **Assigning a Variable to a Specific Metadata Category**

```
$ssApp = Get-SPEnterpriseSearchServiceApplication
-Identity 81aedaf7-704c-47f4-8173-5e99a7495ac3
$category = Get-SPEnterpriseSearchMetadataCategory
-SearchApplication $ssApp -Identity "Custom Properties"
```

Create a Custom Metadata Crawled Property

Scenario/Problem: You want to create a metadata crawled property.

Solution: Use the New-SPEnterpriseSearchMetadataCrawledProperty cmdlet.

Instead of crawling content to generate a crawled property, you can use this search
cmdlet to create a crawled property entry within a search service application. This
makes replicating search configurations within various environments (development,
staging, production, and so on) easier. Listing 13.11 shows sample command lines.

LISTING 13.11 **Creating a New Metadata Crawled Property**

```
$ssApp = Get-SPEnterpriseSearchServiceApplication
-Identity 81aedaf7-704c-47f4-8173-5e99a7495ac3
$category = Get-SPEnterpriseSearchMetadataCategory
-SearchApplication $ssApp -Identity "SharePoint"
New-SPEnterpriseSearchMetadataCrawledProperty -Name "ows_NewField"
-SearchApplication $ssApp -Category $category -VariantType 31
-PropSet 00130329-0000-0130-c000-000000131346   -IsNameEnum $false
```

The VariantType parameter determines the type of data stored within the crawled
property. The valid types and associated values are as follows:

▶ Text: 31

▶ Integer: 20

▶ Date and Time: 64

▶ Yes/No: 11

▶ Binary Data: 12

PropSet is the property set associated with the category and crawled properties. The best way to find the correct property set is to investigate the crawled properties within Central Administration (from Manage Service Applications, select Search Service Application, select Managed Properties, and then click Crawled Properties link at top of screen) or use the Get-SPEnterpriseSearchMetaDataCrawledProperty cmdlet (explained in the next section).

The IsNameEnum switch parameter is required and determines whether the underlying data is actually an integer that is being converted to a string.

> **NOTE** The execution of the commands will state that the SearchApplication parameter is ignored, however, if you do not provide SearchApplication, the cmdlet prompts for the entry.

Display Available Crawled Properties

> **Scenario/Problem:** You want to view the information on the available search metadata crawled properties.

Solution: Use the Get-SPEnterpriseSearchMetadataCrawledProperty cmdlet.

The Get-SPEnterpriseSearchMetaDataCrawledProperty cmdlet provides information on the Enterprise Search metadata categories configured for a particular search service application. Therefore, you need to provide a search service application with this cmdlet, as shown in Listing 13.12.

LISTING 13.12 **Displaying the Search Metadata Categories**

```
$ssApp = Get-SPEnterpriseSearchServiceApplication
-Identity 81aedaf7-704c-47f4-8173-5e99a7495ac3
Get-SPEnterpriseSearchMetadataCrawledProperty
-SearchApplication $ssApp
```

The Enterprise Search Service metadata crawled properties are displayed, as shown in Figure 13.5.

> **TIP** Use the Where-Object clause to limit the amount of crawled properties displayed. Here is an example:
>
> ```
> Get-SPEnterpriseSearchMetadataCrawledProperty —SearchApplication
> $ssApp | Where-Object {$_.CategoryName -eq "SharePoint"}
> ```

FIGURE 13.5 Displaying the Enterprise Search Service application metadata crawled properties.

Get a Specific Metadata Crawled Property

Scenario/Problem: You need to obtain a metadata crawled property reference for use in other search cmdlets.

Solution: Use the Get-SPEnterpriseSearchMetadataCrawledProperty cmdlet to assign a variable the results using the -Identity and -SearchApplication parameters.

Providing the identity of the metadata crawled property with the Get-SPEnterpriseSearchMetadataCrawledProperty cmdlet retrieves a specific metadata crawled property for the specified search service application. Use this to assign the results to an object for use in other cmdlets, as shown in Listing 13.13.

LISTING 13.13 **Assigning a Variable to a Specific Metadata Crawled Property**

```
$ssApp = Get-SPEnterpriseSearchServiceApplication
-Identity 81aedaf7-704c-47f4-8173-5e99a7495ac3
$crawledproperty = Get-SPEnterpriseSearchMetadataCrawledProperty
-SearchApplication $ssApp -Name "ows_NewField"
```

Create a Custom Metadata-Managed Property

Scenario/Problem: You want to create a metadata managed property.

Solution: Use the `New-SPEnterpriseSearchMetadataManagedProperty` cmdlet.

Instead of crawling content to generate a managed property, you can use this search cmdlet to create a managed property entry within a search service application. This makes replicating search configurations within various environments (development, staging, production, and so on) easier. Listing 13.14 shows sample command lines.

LISTING 13.14 **Creating a New Metadata-Managed Property**

```
$ssApp = Get-SPEnterpriseSearchServiceApplication
-Identity 81aedaf7-704c-47f4-8173-5e99a7495ac3
$category = Get-SPEnterpriseSearchMetadataCategory
-SearchApplication $ssApp -Identity "SharePoint"
New-SPEnterpriseSearchMetadataManagedProperty -Name "NewField"
-SearchApplication $ssApp -Type 1
```

The `Type` parameter determines the type of data stored within the managed property. The valid types and values are as follows:

- ▶ `Text:` 1
- ▶ `Integer:` 2
- ▶ `Decimal:` 3
- ▶ `DateTime:` 4
- ▶ `YesNo:` 5
- ▶ `Binary:` 6

Display Available Managed Properties

Scenario/Problem: You want to view the information on the available search metadata managed properties.

Solution: Use the `Get-SPEnterpriseSearchMetadataManagedProperty` cmdlet.

The `Get-SPEnterpriseSearchMetadataManagedProperty` cmdlet provides information on the Enterprise Search metadata categories configured for a particular search service application. Therefore, you need to provide a search service application with this cmdlet, as shown in Listing 13.15.

LISTING 13.15 **Displaying the Search Metadata-Managed Properties**

```
$ssApp = Get-SPEnterpriseSearchServiceApplication
-Identity 81aedaf7-704c-47f4-8173-5e99a7495ac3
Get-SPEnterpriseSearchMetadataManagedProperty
-SearchApplication $ssApp
```

The Enterprise Search Service metadata-managed properties are displayed, as shown in Figure 13.6.

FIGURE 13.6 Displaying the Enterprise Search Service application metadata-managed properties.

Get a Specific Metadata-Managed Property

Scenario/Problem: You need to obtain a metadata managed property reference for use in other search cmdlets.

Solution: Use the `Get-SPEnterpriseSearchMetadataManagedProperty` cmdlet to assign a variable the results using the `-Identity` and `-SearchApplication` parameters.

Providing the identity of the metadata-managed property with the `Get-SPEnterpriseSearchMetadataManagedProperty` cmdlet retrieves a specific metadata-managed property for the specified search service application. Use this to assign the results to an object for use in other cmdlets, as shown in Listing 13.16.

LISTING 13.16 **Assigning a Variable to a Specific Metadata-Managed Property**

```
$ssApp = Get-SPEnterpriseSearchServiceApplication
-Identity 81aedaf7-704c-47f4-8173-5e99a7495ac3
$managedproperty = Get-SPEnterpriseSearchMetadataManagedProperty
-SearchApplication $ssApp -Identity NewField
```

Create a Metadata Mapping

Scenario/Problem: You need to map a crawled property to a managed property.

Solution: Use the New-SPEnterpriseSearchMetadataMapping cmdlet.

To be able to use new search fields within SharePoint, you must map the crawled properties to managed properties. You can use the variables generated in the previous sections to map the two together using the New-SPEnterpriseSearchMetadataMapping cmdlet. Listing 13.17 shows sample command lines.

LISTING 13.17 **Creating a New Metadata Mapping**

```
$ssApp = Get-SPEnterpriseSearchServiceApplication
-Identity 81aedaf7-704c-47f4-8173-5e99a7495ac3
$crawledproperty = Get-SPEnterpriseSearchMetadataCrawledProperty
-SearchApplication $ssApp -Name "ows_NewField"
$managedproperty = Get-SPEnterpriseSearchMetadataManagedProperty
-SearchApplication $ssApp -Identity NewField
New-SPEnterpriseSearchMetadataMapping -SearchApplication $ssApp
-ManagedProperty $managedproperty -CrawledProperty $crawledproperty
```

TIP Change the Get statements to New statements such that you may generate the crawled and managed properties on the fly while performing the mapping.

Use Advanced Cmdlets for Search

Scenario/Problem: You want to script out more detailed steps involving search components such as querying, crawling, and topology.

Solution: Use the cmdlets listed in Appendix C, "Enterprise Search Reference."

This chapter covers the basic or more common cmdlets. For more advanced scripting with Enterprise Search, Appendix C references all the search cmdlets.

CHAPTER 14

Profile Service

This chapter explores the administrative aspects of the User Profile Service through the use of SharePoint PowerShell cmdlets.

Get the Identity of the Profile Service Application

Scenario/Problem: You need to find the identity of the Profile Service Application.

Solution: Use the `Get-SPServiceApplication` cmdlet.

To get a specific instance of a metadata service application, you need the identity of the service application. The `Set-SPProfileServiceApplication` cmdlet requires an `Identity` parameter, but no `Get-SPProfileServiceApplication` cmdlet exists. Therefore, you need to use the `Get-SPServiceApplication` cmdlet to display all service applications and find the User Profile Service. Listing 14.1 shows the command line without any parameters.

LISTING 14.1 **Displaying the List of Service Applications**

```
Get-SPServiceApplication
```

Get a Specific Profile Service Application Instance

Scenario/Problem: You need to obtain a Profile Service application instance reference.

Solution: Use the `Get-SPServiceApplication` cmdlet to assign a variable the results using the `-Identity` parameter.

Providing the identity of the Profile Service Application instance with the `Get-SPServiceApplication` cmdlet retrieves a specific secure store service instance. Use this to assign the results to an object for use in other cmdlets, as shown in Listing 14.2.

LISTING 14.2 **Assigning a Variable to a Specific Metadata Service Application**

```
$profileSA = Get-SPServiceApplication -Identity 9b6235e4-f306-4ccc-
8192-0c83cb679476
```

No cmdlet exists for getting an object type related to a user profile service application. Any cmdlet using the service application identity uses the

SPServiceApplicationPipeBind type, so a generic service application object needs to be utilized.

Configure Settings on the Profile Service Application

Scenario/Problem: You want to configure settings on the Profile Service.

Solution: Use the Set-SPProfileServiceApplication cmdlet with an Identity variable.

You can use the Set-SPProfileServiceApplication cmdlet to configure settings on the profile service application using an Identity variable, as shown in Listing 14.3.

LISTING 14.3 **Configuring the Profile Service Settings**

```
$profileSA = Get-SPServiceApplication -Identity 9b6235e4-f306-4ccc-
8192-0c83cb679476
Set-SPProfileServiceApplication -Identity $profileSA
-MySiteHostLocation http://sp2013:80/my/ -MySiteManagedPath my/personal
```

The Set-SPProfileServiceApplication cmdlet has two similar parameter sets. In addition to the MySite parameters, you can configure various DB credentials. Run Set-SPProfileServiceApplication -? to review additional parameters.

Remove Old Comments

Scenario/Problem: You want to remove comments from the Profile Service Application.

Solution: Use the Remove-SPSocialItemByDate cmdlet with the RemoveComments parameter.

The Remove-SPSocialItemByDate cmdlet enables you to remove comments, tags, or ratings before a particular required end date. Listing 14.4 shows an example command line.

LISTING 14.4 **Removing Old Comments from the Profile Service**

```
$profileProxy = Get-SPServiceApplicationProxy -Identity 150232e4-a3d2-
4915-adb1-155ea77a6dfb
Remove-SPSocialItemByDate -ProfileServiceApplicationProxy
$profileProxy -RemoveComments:$true -EndDate 12/1/2013 -Confirm:$false
```

RemoveComments is a Boolean parameter, although it looks like a switch parameter. Therefore, either $true or $false needs to be provided as the Boolean value. The service application proxy for the User Profile Service is needed and can be obtained by reviewing the output from Get-SPServiceApplicationProxy.

Remove Old Ratings

Scenario/Problem: You want to remove comments from the Profile Service Application.

Solution: Use the Remove-SPSocialItemByDate cmdlet with the RemoveRatings parameter.

The Remove-SPSocialItemByDate cmdlet enables you to remove comments, tags, or ratings before a particular required end date. Listing 14.5 shows an example command line.

LISTING 14.5 **Removing Old Ratings from the Profile Service**

```
$profileProxy = Get-SPServiceApplicationProxy -Identity 150232e4-a3d2-
4915-adb1-155ea77a6dfb
Remove-SPSocialItemByDate -ProfileServiceApplicationProxy
$profileProxy -RemoveRatings:$true -EndDate 12/1/2013 -Confirm:$false
```

RemoveRatings is a Boolean parameter, although it looks like a switch parameter. Therefore, either $true or $false needs to be provided as the Boolean value. The service application proxy for the User Profile Service is needed and can be obtained by reviewing the output from Get-SPServiceApplicationProxy.

Remove Old Tags

Scenario/Problem: You want to remove comments from the Profile Service Application.

Solution: Use the Remove-SPSocialItemByDate cmdlet with the RemoveTags parameter.

The Remove-SPSocialItemByDate cmdlet enables you to remove comments, tags, or ratings before a particular required end date. Listing 14.6 shows an example command line.

LISTING 14.6 **Removing Old Tags from the Profile Service**

```
$profileProxy = Get-SPServiceApplicationProxy -Identity 150232e4-a3d2-
4915-adb1-155ea77a6dfb
Remove-SPSocialItemByDate -ProfileServiceApplicationProxy $profileProxy
-RemoveTags:$true -EndDate 12/1/2013 -Confirm:$false
```

RemoveTags is a Boolean parameter, although it looks like a switch parameter.
Therefore, either $true or $false needs to be provided as the Boolean value. The
service application proxy for the User Profile Service is needed and can be obtained by
reviewing the output from Get-SPServiceApplicationProxy.

Update the Profile Photo Store

> **Scenario/Problem:** You upgraded to SharePoint 2010 and need to update the
> Profile Photo Store.

Solution: Use the Update-SPProfilePhotoStore cmdlet with the
MySiteHostLocation parameter.

After you upgrade from MOSS 2007 to SharePoint 2013, you need to ensure that
the profile photo store is compatible with SharePoint 2013. Using the Update-
SPProfilePhotoStore cmdlet, shown in Listing 14.7, ensures that the photo store is
updated accordingly.

```
Update-SPProfilePhotoStore -MySiteHostLocation http://mysites
```

LISTING 14.7 **Removing Old Tags from the Profile Service**

```
Update-SPProfilePhotoStore -MySiteHostLocation http://mysites
```

Refresh the Feed Cache

> **Scenario/Problem:** The feed cache timer job failed and you need to refresh the
> feed cache.

Solution: Use the Update-SPRepopulateMicroblogLMTCache cmdlet.

To refresh the feed cache with the last modified times, execute the Update-
SPRepopulateMicroblogLMTCache cmdlet using the Profile Service Application
Proxy, as shown in Listing 14.8.

LISTING 14.8 **Update the Feed Cache**

```
$profileProxy = Get-SPServiceApplicationProxy -Identity 150232e4-a3d2-
4915-adb1-155ea77a6dfb

Update-SPRepopulateMicroblogLMTCache -ProfileServiceApplicationProxy
$profileProxy
```

Refresh a Specific User's Feed Cache

Scenario/Problem: A user's feed cache is not being refreshed or updated with the latest statuses.

Solution: Use the Update-SPRepopulateMicroblogFeedCache cmdlet.

To refresh the feed cache of a specific user, execute the Update-SPRepopulateMicroblogFeedCache cmdlet using the user's account and the Profile Service Application Proxy, as shown in Listing 14.9.

LISTING 14.9 **Update the Feed Cache**

```
$profileProxy = Get-SPServiceApplicationProxy -Identity 150232e4-a3d2-
4915-adb1-155ea77a6dfb

Update-SPRepopulateMicroblogLMTCache -AccountName "SP\FeedUser"
-ProfileServiceApplicationProxy $profileProxy
```

Use Advanced Cmdlets for the Profile Service

Scenario/Problem: You need to use more advanced cmdlets for the Profile Service.

Solution: Use the cmdlets listed in this section.

This chapter covers the basic or more common cmdlets for the Profile Service. For more advanced scripting, the following cmdlet nouns are also available:

▸ SPSiteSubscriptionProfileConfig

▸ SPProfileServiceApplicationSecurity

▸ SPProfileServiceApplicationProxy

- SPProfileLeader
- SPProfilePropertyCollection
- SPProfileServiceFullReplication
- SPProfileServiceRecoveryReplication
- SPProfileServiceIncrementalReplication

CHAPTER 15

Business Data Connectivity Service

This chapter explores the administrative aspects of the Business Data Connectivity Service (BCS) through the use of SharePoint PowerShell cmdlets. BCS is the replacement of the Business Data Catalog (BDC) from MOSS 2007, although there are remnants of the reference to the Business Data Catalog.

Get the Identity of the BCS Service Application

Scenario/Problem: You need to find the identity of the BCS Service Application.

Solution: Use the `Get-SPServiceApplication` cmdlet.

To get a specific instance of a metadata service application, you need the identity of the service application. The `Set-SPBusinessDataCatalogServiceApplication` cmdlet requires an `Identity` parameter, but no `Get-SPBusinessDataCatalogServiceApplication` cmdlet exists. Therefore, you need to use the `Get-SPServiceApplication` cmdlet to display all service applications and find the Business Data Connectivity Service. Listing 15.1 shows the command line without any parameters.

LISTING 15.1 **Displaying the List of Service Applications**

```
Get-SPServiceApplication
```

Get a Specific BCS Service Application Instance

Scenario/Problem: You need to obtain a Secure Store Service application instance reference.

Solution: Use the `Get-SPServiceApplication` cmdlet to assign a variable the results using the `-Identity` parameter.

Providing the identity of the Business Data Connectivity `ServiceApplication` instance with the `Get-SPServiceApplication` cmdlet retrieves a specific Business Data Connectivity Service instance. Use this to assign the results to an object for use in other cmdlets, as shown in Listing 15.2.

LISTING 15.2 **Assigning a Variable to a Business Data Service Application**

```
$bcs = Get-SPServiceApplication -Identity b7b3652e-6f51-4161-935a-
0631a1100ecf
```

No cmdlet exists for getting get an object type related to a Business Data Connectivity Service application. Any cmdlet using the service application identity uses the SPServiceApplicationPipeBind type, so a generic service application object needs to be utilized.

Configure the BCS Database

Scenario/Problem: You want to use a new database for the BCS service application.

Solution: Use the Set-SPBusinessDataCatalogServiceApplication cmdlet with the DatabaseName parameter.

When the Business Data Connectivity Service Application is created, by default, the database name is Bdc_Service_DB_<guid>. You can easily change this to a new database using the DatabaseName parameter with the Set-SPBusinessDataCatalog ServiceApplication cmdlet, as shown in Listing 15.3.

LISTING 15.3 **Configuring a New Database for BCS**

```
$bcs = Get-SPServiceApplication -Identity b7b3652e-6f51-4161-935a-
0631a1100ecf
Set-SPBusinessDataCatalogServiceApplication -Identity $bcs -DatabaseName
BCS_DB
```

If the database does not exist, a new database is created. Simply drop the old one with the GUID in the name and make your DBAs happy. By default, the database server is assumed to be the SQL Server instance that SharePoint is using. You can specify the database server by using the -DatabaseServer parameter. You need to specify the database credentials only if SQL authentication is being used.

Get a BCS Metadata Object

Scenario/Problem: You need to obtain a BCS metatdata object reference.

Solution: Use the Get-SPBusinessDataCatalogMetadataObject cmdlet.

To perform import and export operations, you need the related meta-data object that stores or will store the BCS entity. Use the Get-SPBusinessDataCatalogMetadataObject cmdlet to set a variable to the meta-data object, as shown in Listing 15.4.

LISTING 15.4 **Getting a BCS Metadata Object**

```
$bcsMeta = Get-SPBusinessDataCatalogMetadataObject -ServiceContext
http://sp2013 -BDCObjectType Catalog -Name ApplicationRegistry
```

The BDCObjectType can be one of the following values:

- ▶ Catalog
- ▶ Model
- ▶ LobSystem
- ▶ LobSystemInstance
- ▶ Entity

The Name parameter might be required, based on the BDCObjectType that is referenced.

Import a BCS Model

Scenario/Problem: You need to import a BCS model.

Solution: Use the Import-SPBusinessDataCatalogModel cmdlet.

The Import-SPBusinessDataCatalogModel cmdlet enables you to import a model file from a local or shared drive. Use a BCS metadata object variable as the Identity, as shown in Listing 15.5.

LISTING 15.5 **Importing a BCS Model**

```
Import-SPBusinessDataCatalogModel -Identity $bcsMeta -Path E:\BCS_Model.
bdcm
```

Several optional switch parameters can be used:

- ▶ Force: Forces an overwrite if the model exists
- ▶ ModelsIncluded: Specifies that models are included in the imported XML file
- ▶ PermissionsIncluded: Specifies that the permissions to the model are included
- ▶ PropertiesIncluded: Specifies that BCS properties are included

Export a BCS Model

> **Scenario/Problem:** You need to export a BCS model.

Solution: Use the `Export-SPBusinessDataCatalogModel` cmdlet.

The `Export-SPBusinessDataCatalogModel` cmdlet enables you to export a model file to a local or shared drive. Use a BCS metadata object variable as the `Identity`, as shown in Listing 15.6.

LISTING 15.6 **Exporting a BCS Model**

```
$bcsMeta = Get-SPBusinessDataCatalogMetadataObject -ServiceContext
http://sp2013 -BDCObjectType Catalog -Name ApplicationRegistry
Export-SPBusinessDataCatalogModel -Identity $bcsMeta -Path E:\BCS_Model.
bdcm
```

Several optional switch parameters can be used:

- ▶ `Force`: Forces the overwriting of a file if the output file exists
- ▶ `ModelsIncluded`: Specifies that models are included in the exported XML file
- ▶ `PermissionsIncluded`: Specifies that the permissions to the model are included in the export
- ▶ `PropertiesIncluded`: Specifies that BCS properties are included in the export
- ▶ `ProxiesIncluded`: Specifies that proxy information for the BCS service application is included in the export.

Set the Entity Notification Web

> **Scenario/Problem:** You need to set up the entity notification web for Business Connectivity services.

Solution: Use the `Set-SPBusinessDataCatalogEntityNotificationWeb` cmdlet.

The `Set-SPBusinessDataCatalogEntityNotificationWeb` cmdlet enables you to specify a SharePoint web as the entity notification web. Use the web object variable or URL for the `-Web` parameter. as shown in Listing 15.7.

LISTING 15.7 **Setting the Entity Notification Web**

```
Set-SPBusinessDataCatalogEntityNotificationWeb -Web "http://sp2013"
```

Get the Entity Notification Web

Scenario/Problem: You need to retrieve an entity notification web object for Business Connectivity services.

Solution: Use the `Get-SPBusinessDataCatalogEntityNotificationWeb` cmdlet.

The `Get-SPBusinessDataCatalogEntityNotificationWeb` cmdlet retrieves the entity notification web for the provided service context. Use a service context object variable or web application URL for the `-ServiceContext` parameter, as shown in Listing 15.8.

LISTING 15.8 **Getting the Entity Notification Web**

```
Get-SPBusinessDataCatalogEntityNotificationWeb
-ServiceContext "http://sp2013"
```

Create an OData Connection

Scenario/Problem: You would like to create an OData connection for Business Connectivity Services.

Solution: Use the `New-SPODataConnectionSetting` cmdlet.

The `New-SPODataConnectionSetting` cmdlet enables you to create OData connections for Business Connectivity Services, which can be internal or external. Listing 15.9 shows an example.

LISTING 15.9 **Creating an OData Connection for BCS**

```
New-SPODataConnectionSetting -Name "PhillyBikeNetwork"
-ServiceContext "http://sp2013"
 -ServiceAddressUrl
"http://gis.phila.gov/ArcGIS/rest/services/PhilaOITGIS_Transportation/
MapServer?f=json&pretty=true"
-AuthenticationMode Anonymous
```

Successful execution of this cmdlet presents the new OData Connection Settings, as shown in Figure 15.1. The `AuthenticationMode` parameter can be any of the following values:

▶ Force

▶ PassThrough

▶ RevertToSelf

▶ Credentials

▶ WindowsCredentials

▶ DigestCredentials

▶ ClientCertificate

▶ Anonymous

FIGURE 15.1 Creating an OData Connection Setting.

If credentials are required, you can set them up using the Secure Store Service and then provide the secure store application ID to the cmdlet using the -SecureStoreTargetApplicationID parameter.

Get an OData Connection

Scenario/Problem: You need to create an OData Connection settings object for use in other cmdlets.

Solution: Use the Get-SPODataConnectionSetting cmdlet.

The Get-SPODataConnectionSetting cmdlet enables you to retrieve OData connection settings. Provide the name of the connection and service context to identity the specific connection. Use a variable to store the settings, as shown in Listing 15.10. You can then use the variable in other cmdlets (see the next section for an example).

LISTING 15.10 **Getting a Specific OData Connection for BCS**

```
$odata = Get-SPODataConnectionSetting -Name "PhillyBikeNetwork"
-ServiceContext "http://sp2013"
```

Update an OData Connection

Scenario/Problem: You need to make a change to an existing OData connec-tion for Business Connectivity Services.

Solution: Use the Set-SPODataConnectionSetting cmdlet.

The Set-SPODataConnectionSetting cmdlet enables you to update existing OData connections for Business Connectivity Services. You simply use the Name of the connection as shown in Listing 15.11 or provide an OData Connection setting object using the Identity parameter, as shown in Listing 15.12.

LISTING 15.11 **Updating an OData Connection for BCS Using the Name**

```
Set-SPODataConnectionSetting -Name "PhillyBikeNetwork"
-ServiceContext "http://sp2013"
 -ServiceAddressUrl
"http://gis.phila.gov/ArcGIS/rest/services/PhilaOITGIS_Transportation/
MapServer?f=json&pretty=true"
-AuthenticationMode Anonymous
```

LISTING 15.12 **Updating an OData Connection for BCS Using the Identity**

```
$odata = Get-SPODataConnectionSetting -Name "PhillyBikeNetwork"
-ServiceContext "http://sp2013"

Set-SPODataConnectionSetting -Identity $odata
-ServiceContext "http://sp2013"
 -ServiceAddressUrl
"http://gis.phila.gov/ArcGIS/rest/services/PhilaOITGIS_Transportation/
MapServer?f=json&pretty=true"
-AuthenticationMode Anonymous
```

If you do not use the -Confim parameter, you are prompted to confirm the update, as shown in Figure 15.2.

FIGURE 15.2 Updating an OData Connection Setting.

CHAPTER 16

Secure Store Service

This chapter explores the administrative aspects of the Secure Store Service through the use of SharePoint PowerShell cmdlets. Only a few cmdlets are used for the actual service application (SPSecureStoreServiceApplication); most of the cmdlets are used for a specific application (SPSecureStoreApplication) that is being secured by the Secure Store Service.

Get the Identity of the Secure Store Service Application

Scenario/Problem: You need to find the identity of the Secure Store Service Application.

Solution: Use the Get-SPServiceApplication cmdlet.

To get a specific instance of a metadata service application, you need the identity of the service application. The Set-SPSecureStoreServiceApplication cmdlet requires an Identity parameter, but no Get-SPSecureStoreServiceApplication cmdlet exists. Therefore, you need to use the Get-SPServiceApplication cmdlet to display all service applications and find the Secure Store Service. Listing 16.1 shows the command line without any parameters.

LISTING 16.1 **Displaying the List of Service Applications**

```
Get-SPServiceApplication
```

Get a Specific Secure Store Service Application Instance

Scenario/Problem: You need to obtain a Secure Store Service application instance reference.

Solution: Use the Get-SPServiceApplication cmdlet to assign a variable the results using the -Identity parameter.

Providing the identity of the Secure Store Service Application instance with the Get-SPServiceApplication cmdlet retrieves a specific Secure Store Service instance. Use this to assign the results to an object for use in other cmdlets, as shown in Listing 16.2.

LISTING 16.2 **Assigning a Variable to a Specific Metadata Service Application**

```
$sss = Get-SPServiceApplication -Identity bc4399ed-a2e0-4397-bf07-
cd3d207e630e
```

No cmdlet exists for getting an object type related to a Secure Store Service application. Any cmdlet using the service application identity uses the SPServiceApplicationPipeBind type, so a generic service application object needs to be utilized.

Enable Auditing for the Secure Store Service

Scenario/Problem: You want to enable auditing for the Secure Store Service.

Solution: Use the Set-SPSecureStoreServiceApplication cmdlet with the audit parameters.

Two audit parameters can be used with the Set-SPSecureStoreServiceApplication cmdlet. The first parameter, AuditingEnabled, is a switch parameter that determines whether auditing is enabled. The second parameter, AuditlogMaxSize, determines how many days to retain the logs. Listing 16.3 shows example command lines.

LISTING 16.3 **Configuring the Secure Store Service Auditing**

```
$sss = Get-SPServiceApplication -Identity bc4399ed-a2e0-4397-bf07-
cd3d207e630e
Set-SPSecureStoreServiceApplication -Identity $sss -AuditingEnabled
-AuditlogMaxSize 15
```

TIP To disable auditing, use —AuditingEnabled:$false.

Auditing is disabled by default; the initial retention value is 30 days.

Configure the Secure Store Database

Scenario/Problem: You want to use a new database for the secure store service application.

Solution: Use the Set-SPSecureStoreServiceApplication cmdlet with the DatabaseName parameter.

When the Secure Store Service Application is created, by default, the database name is `Secure_Store_Service_<guid>`. You can easily change this to a new database using the `DatabaseName` parameter with the `Set-SPSecureStoreServiceApplication` cmdlet, as shown in Listing 16.4.

LISTING 16.4 **Configuring a New Database for the Secure Store**

```
$sss = Get-SPServiceApplication -Identity bc4399ed-a2e0-4397-bf07-
cd3d207e630e
Set-SPSecureStoreServiceApplication -Identity $sss -DatabaseName
SecureStoreDB
```

If the database does not exist, a new database is created. Simply drop the old one with the GUID in the name and make your DBAs happy. By default, the database server is assumed to be the SQL Server instance that SharePoint is using. You can specify the database server using the `-DatabaseServer` parameter. You need to specify the database credentials only if SQL authentication is being used.

> **NOTE** At the time of this writing, a new database is only being created when a new database name is specified from within Central Administration. Although the PowerShell cmdlet changes the name, the new database does not appear in SQL Server. However, reviewing the properties of the Secure Store Service Application and clicking OK does indeed create the new database.

Generate a New Master Key

> **Scenario/Problem:** You need to create or change the master key for the Secure Store Service.

Solution: Use the `Update-SPSecureStoreMasterKey` cmdlet.

The Secure Store Service needs a master key before target applications can be created. To create or change the master key, use the `Update-SPSecureStoreMasterKey`, as shown in Listing 16.5.

LISTING 16.5 **Generating a New Master Key**

```
Update-SPSecureStoreMasterKey -ServiceApplicationProxy da9247cb-9055-
4024-817c-714ef98656e1 -PassPhrase SharePoint1
```

This cmdlet requires the service application proxy GUID for the Secure Store Service. To find the GUID, use the `Get-SPServiceApplicationProxy` cmdlet and locate the

Secure Store Service entry. The display name cannot be used here. The passphrase is a plain-text entry and does not need to be encrypted.

Refresh the Encryption Key

Scenario/Problem: You need to create or propagate the master key to all application servers.

Solution: Use the `Update-SPSecureStoreApplicationServerKey` cmdlet.

After a master key (encryption key) is created or updated, all application servers need to be aware of the key. You can propagate the encryption key to all application servers by using the `Update-SPSecureStoreApplicationServerKey` cmdlet, as shown in Listing 16.6.

LISTING 16.6 **Propagating the Encryption Key to All Application Servers**

```
Update-SPSecureStoreApplicationServerKey -ServiceApplicationProxy
da9247cb-9055-4024-817c-714ef98656e1 -PassPhrase SharePoint1
```

This cmdlet requires the service application proxy GUID for the Secure Store Service. To find the GUID, use the `Get-SPServiceApplicationProxy` cmdlet and locate the Secure Store Service entry. The display name cannot be used here. The passphrase is a plain-text entry and does not need to be encrypted, but it must match the passphrase used when the master key was created.

Create Application Fields

Scenario/Problem: You need to create field variables for use in creating a new application in the Secure Store Service.

Solution: Use the `New-SPSecureStoreApplicationField` cmdlet.

When creating a new application for the Secure Store Service, several application fields are needed. These application fields can be created using the `New-SPSecureStoreApplicationField` cmdlet. The types of fields are as follows:

- `Username`
- `Password`
- `WindowsUsername`
- `WindowsPassword`

▶ Key

▶ Pin

▶ Generic

Typically, you use the Secure Store Service to provide single sign-on functionality using a dedicated service account that has access to the application. Therefore, the most common field types are `WindowsUsername` and `WindowsPassword`. Use variables to create and store these fields, as shown in Listing 16.7, such that the variables may be reused when creating a new application entry.

LISTING 16.7 **Creating Application Fields**

```
$windowsUser = New-SPSecureStoreApplicationField -Name "SP\AppSvcAccount"
-Type WindowsUserName -Masked:$false
$windowsPass = New-SPSecureStoreApplicationField -Name "password" -Type
WindowsPassword -Masked:$true
```

The `Masked` switch parameter is required and, therefore, must have a `$true` or `$false` value. This determines whether the field text entry should be masked, as is the case with passwords.

When using the fields, stored in variables, within other cmdlets, the variables need to be combined, as shown in Listing 16.8.

LISTING 16.8 **Combining Application Fields**

```
$appFields = $windowsUser, $windowsPass
```

Combining the fields produces a fields array, shown in Figure 16.1. Other cmdlets, such as `New-SPSecureStoreApplication`, require this.

FIGURE 16.1 Reviewing the contents of a fields array.

Create a Target Application

Scenario/Problem: You need to create a new application entry and need a target application variable.

Solution: Use the `New-SPSecureStoreTargetApplication` cmdlet.

When creating a new application for the Secure Store Service, you must specify the target application. You can create the target application object using the `New-SPSecureStoreTargetApplication` cmdlet. You configure the type of application using the `ApplicationType` parameter and one of the following values:

- `Individual`
- `Group`
- `IndividualWithTicketing`
- `GroupWithTicketing`
- `RestrictedIndividual`
- `RestrictedGroup`

Typically, you are using the Secure Store Service to provide single sign-on functionality using a dedicated service account that has access to the application. Therefore, the most common application type is `Group`. Use a variable to create the target application object, as shown in Listing 16.9, so that the object can be used when creating a new application entry.

LISTING 16.9 **Creating the Target Application**

```
$targetApp = New-SPSecureStoreTargetApplication -Name "SSOApplication"
-FriendlyName "SSO Application" -ApplicationType Group
```

The `Name` entry becomes the `ApplicationID` for the Secure Store Service application; therefore, providing a name without spaces is recommended. Use the `FriendlyName` parameter to provide a proper display name.

Create a New Application Entry

Scenario/Problem: You need to create a new application entry to the Secure Store Service.

Solution: Use the `New-SPSecureStoreApplication` cmdlet.

Creating a new application entry essentially combines several of the previous sections into one script so that the `New-SPSecureStoreApplication` cmdlet has the necessary values. This involves the target application and application field objects, as shown in Listing 16.10.

LISTING 16.10 **Creating the Secure Store Application Entry**

```
$windowsUser = New-SPSecureStoreApplicationField -Name "SP\AppSvcAccount"
-Type WindowsUserName -Masked:$false

$windowsPass = New-SPSecureStoreApplicationField -Name "password" -Type
WindowsPassword -Masked:$true

$appFields = $windowsUser, $windowsPass

$targetApp = New-SPSecureStoreTargetApplication -Name "SSOApplication"
-FriendlyName "SSO Application" -ApplicationType Group

New-SPSecureStoreApplication -ServiceContext http://sp2013
-TargetApplication $targetApp -Fields $appFields
```

NOTE Even though the Administrator parameter is optional, it may be required depending on the target application configuration.

CHAPTER 17

Metadata Service

This chapter explores the administrative aspects of the Managed Metadata Service through the use of SharePoint PowerShell cmdlets.

Get the Identity of the Metadata Service Application

Scenario/Problem: You need to find the identity of the Metadata Service Application.

Solution: Use the `Get-SPServiceApplication` cmdlet.

To get a specific instance of a metadata service application, you need the identity of the service application. The `Get-SPMetadataServiceApplication` cmdlet requires an `Identity` parameter and, therefore, does not display all instances. Therefore, you need to use the `Get-SPServiceApplication` cmdlet to display all service applications and find the Managed Metadata Service. Listing 17.1 shows the command line without any parameters.

LISTING 17.1 **Displaying the List of Service Applications**

```
Get-SPServiceApplication
```

Get a Specific Metadata Service Application Instance

Scenario/Problem: You need to obtain a metadata service application instance reference.

Solution: Use the `Get-SPMetadataServiceApplication` cmdlet to assign a variable the results using the `-Identity` parameter.

Providing the identity of the Metadata Service Application instance with the `Get-SPMetadataServiceApplication` cmdlet retrieves a specific metadata service instance. Use this to assign the results to an object for use in other cmdlets, as shown in Listing 17.2.

LISTING 17.2 **Assigning a Variable to a Specific Metadata Service Application**

```
$metadataApp = Get-SPMetadataServiceApplication -Identity f3e6d88a-
e0a7-455c-bbef-b4942e7607b5
```

Instead of the GUID, you can use the display name. The default display name for the managed metadata service application is `Managed Metadata Service`. Because this is a long name, when displaying the service applications, the full text is cut off.

Configure the Metadata Service Accounts

Scenario/Problem: You need to configure the service accounts for the metadata application service.

Solution: Use the `Set-SPMetadataServiceApplication` cmdlet with the account parameters.

The Metadata Service Application has four service account setting parameters:

- `AdministratorAccount`
- `FullAccessAccount`
- `RestrictedAccount`
- `ReadAccessAccount`

When setting one of these parameters, the others are removed. Therefore, setting all account parameters at the same time is recommended, as shown in Listing 17.3.

LISTING 17.3 **Configuring the Metadata Service Accounts**

```
Set-SPMetadataServiceApplication -Identity "Managed Metadata Service"
-AdministratorAccount "SP\Administrator" -FullAccessAccount
"SP\MDSFullAccess" -RestrictedAccount "SP\MDSRestricted"
-ReadAccessAccount "SP\ReadAccess1,SP\ReadAccess2"
```

You can specify multiple accounts by providing a comma-separated list of the accounts. All accounts specified must exist in the domain.

Configure the Term Store Database

Scenario/Problem: You want to use a new database for the metadata service application.

Solution: Use the `Set-SPMetadataServiceApplication` cmdlet with the `DatabaseName` parameter.

When the Metadata Service Application is created, by default, the database name is
`Managed Metadata Service_<guid>`. You can easily change this to a new database
using the `DatabaseName` parameter with the `Set-SPMetadataServiceApplication`
cmdlet, as shown in Listing 17.4.

LISTING 17.4 **Configuring the Term Store Database**

```
Set-SPMetadataServiceApplication -Identity "Managed Metadata Service"
-DatabaseName TermStoreDB
```

If the database does not exist, a new database is created. Simply drop the old one with
the GUID in the name and make your DBAs happy. By default, the database server is
assumed to be the SQL Server instance SharePoint is using. You can specify the data-
base server by using the `-DatabaseServer` parameter.

Configure the Content Type Hub

Scenario/Problem: You need to set or change the content type hub which
should be used by the metadata service application.

Solution: Use the `Set-SPMetadataServiceApplication` cmdlet with the `HubUri`
parameter.

The content type hub is the site collection you want to use as your main content
type gallery. The metadata service application uses the specified content type hub to
consume the content types that exist within the site collection. You can set the content
type hub using the `HubUri` parameter with the `Set-SPMetadataServiceApplication`
cmdlet, as shown in Listing 17.5.

LISTING 17.5 **Configuring the Content Type Hub**

```
Set-SPMetadataServiceApplication -Identity "Managed Metadata Service"
-HubUri "http://sp2013"
```

When changing content type hubs, any content type packages are unpublished from the
old location. Use the `DoNotUnpublishAllPackages` switch parameter to specify that
the content type packages should not be unpublished when the content type hub setting
is modified.

Get the Identity of the Metadata Service Application Proxy

Scenario/Problem: You need to find the identity of the Metadata Service Proxy.

Solution: Use the `Get-SPServiceApplicationProxy` cmdlet.

To get a specific instance of a Metadata Service Application Proxy, you need the identity of the Service Application Proxy. The `Get-SPMetadataServiceApplicationProxy` cmdlet requires an `Identity` parameter and, therefore, does not display all instances. Therefore, you need to use the `Get-SPServiceApplicationProxy` cmdlet to display all service application proxies and find the Managed Metadata Service. Listing 17.6 shows the command line without any parameters.

LISTING 17.6 **Displaying the List of Service Application Proxies**

```
Get-SPServiceApplicationProxy
```

NOTE Even though the list of proxies looks identical to the service applications, the GUIDs are different. You need to know the metadata service proxy for certain configuration operations described in this chapter.

Get a Specific Metadata Service Application Proxy Instance

Scenario/Problem: You need to obtain a metadata service application proxy instance reference.

Solution: Use the `Get-SPMetadataServiceApplicationProxy` cmdlet to assign a variable the results using the `-Identity` parameter.

Providing the identity of the proxy with the `Get-SPMetadataServiceApplicationProxy` cmdlet retrieves a specific Metadata Service Application Proxy instance. Use this to assign the results to an object for use in other cmdlets, as shown in Listing 17.7.

LISTING 17.7 **Assigning a Variable to a Specific Metadata Service Application Proxy**

```
$metadataProxy = Get-SPMetadataServiceApplication Proxy -Identity
f3e6d88a-e0a7-455c-bbef-b4942e7607b5
```

Instead of the GUID, you can use the display name. The default display name for the managed metadata service application proxy is `Managed Metadata Service`. Because this is a long name, when displaying the service application proxiess, the full text is cut off.

Configure the Metadata Service Connection Options

Scenario/Problem: You need to set the metadata service connection options.

Solution: Use the `Set-SPMetadataServiceApplicationProxy` cmdlet with the option switch parameters.

The metadata service connection settings are configured at the proxy level. Modifying the properties of the metadata service proxy allows for four settings, as in Figure 17.1.

TIP To get to these properties, from Central Administration, click on the Manage service applications link under Application Management. Locate the Managed Metadata Service entry and highlight the connection (the indented instance). Click on the Properties button from the top ribbon bar.

FIGURE 17.1 Editing the Managed Metadata Service Connection.

These four options are synonymous with the following switch parameters of the `Set-SPMetadataServiceApplicationProxy` cmdlet, respectively:

- ▶ `DefaultKeywordTaxonomy`
- ▶ `DefaultSiteCollectionTaxonomy`

▶ `ContentTypeSyndicationEnabled`

▶ `ContentTypePushdownEnabled`

Use these switch parameters with `$true` or `$false` settings (no setting assumes `true`), as shown in Listing 17.8.

LISTING 17.8 **Configuring the Metadata Service Connection Options**

```
Set-SPMetadataServiceApplicationProxy -Identity "Managed Metadata
Service" -DefaultKeywordTaxonomy -DefaultSiteCollectionTaxonomy
-ContentTypeSyndicationEnabled:$false
-ContentTypePushdownEnabled:$false
```

CHAPTER 18

Session State and State Service

This chapter explores the administrative aspects of the Session State Service and the State Service Application through the use of SharePoint PowerShell cmdlets.

Enable Session State

Scenario/Problem: You want to enable session state for your SharePoint Web Applications.

Solution: Use the `Enable-SPSessionStateService` cmdlet.

The Session State Service is not enabled by default, so there is no database to manage session state. This is actually the ASP.NET session state that can be leveraged by the SharePoint web applications in your farm.

To enable session state, execute the `Enable-SPSessionStateService` cmdlet with the `DefaultProvision` parameter. This automatically creates the session state database and enables the service using default values. Listing 18.1 shows an example command line.

LISTING 18.1 **Enabling Session State Using Defaults**

```
Enable-SPSessionStateService -DefaultProvision
```

The default database is named `SessionStateService_<guid>`. To make sure that the GUID-based name is not used, you can alternatively provide the database name and server using the `Enable-SPSessionStateService` cmdlet, as shown in Listing 18.2.

LISTING 18.2 **Enabling Session State with a Specific Database**

```
Enable-SPSessionStateService -DatabaseName SessionStateDB
-DatabaseServer SP2013\SQLSharePoint
```

NOTE Session state will be enabled across the entire farm, however, in order for the web applications to use session state, each web.config must be modified such that the enableSessionState property of the <pages> element is set to true.

Disable Session State

Scenario/Problem: You want to disable session state for your SharePoint Web Applications.

Solution: Use the `Disable-SPSessionStateService` cmdlet.

Disabling the session state can be performed using the `Disable-SPSessionStateService` cmdlet. Executing this cmdlet removes the current database and disables the service. Listing 18.3 shows an example command line.

LISTING 18.3 **Disabling Session State**

```
Disable-SPSessionStateService
```

Display Session State Information

Scenario/Problem: You want to view the current session state configuration for your SharePoint farm.

Solution: Use the `Get-SPSessionStateService` cmdlet.

The `Get-SPSessionStateService` cmdlet provides the current information regarding session state within your SharePoint farm. Execute the cmdlet with no parameters, as shown in Listing 18.4. If the Session State Service is enabled, the database information is displayed, as shown in Figure 18.1. If the Session State Service is not enabled, the database information is blank, as shown in Figure 18.2 (this is the default after installing a new farm).

LISTING 18.4 **Reviewing the Session State Configuration**

```
Get-SPSessionStateService
```

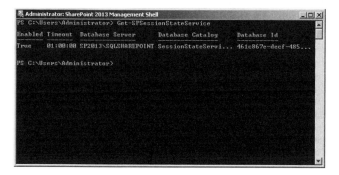

FIGURE 18.1 Displaying an enabled session state configuration.

FIGURE 18.2 Displaying a disabled session state configuration.

Configure the Timeout of the Session State

Scenario/Problem: You need to modify the timeout of the Session State Service.

Solution: Use the `Set-SPSessionStateService` cmdlet with the `SessionTimeout` parameter.

One of the only configuration changes you can perform on the Session State Service is changing the timeout value. When viewing the session state configuration (as explained in the previous section), you notice that the timeout defaults to one hour (01:00:00). To modify this setting, use the `SessionTimeout` parameter with the `Set-SPSessionStateService`, as shown in Listing 18.5.

LISTING 18.5 **Decreasing the Session Timeout to 30 Minutes**

```
Set-SPSessionStateService -SessionTimeout 30
```

The `SessionTimeout` parameter determines the time, in minutes, when an inactive session should be closed or terminated. The default is 60 minutes, but some organizations want to be aggressive and use a lower number such as 20 or 30.

TIP Even though a timeout value is displayed when the session state service is disabled, you may not modify the timeout setting if there is no session state service enabled.

Display State Service Applications Configured on the Farm

Scenario/Problem: You need to obtain the identity of the State Service Application(s) running on your SharePoint farm.

Solution: Use the `Get-SPStateServiceApplication` cmdlet without any parameters to retrieve all available content deployment paths.

To obtain a State Service Application reference object, you need to find the identity of the path entry. Use the `Get-SPStateServiceApplication` by itself, as shown in Listing 18.6, to list all available State Service Applications.

LISTING 18.6 **Display All Available State Service Applications**

```
Get-SPStateServiceApplication
```

Get a Specific State Service Application

Scenario/Problem: You need to obtain a specific State Service Application reference.

Solution: Use the `Get-SPStateServiceApplication` cmdlet to assign a variable the results using the `-Identity` parameter.

Providing the identity of the State Service Application with the `Get-SPStateServiceApplication` cmdlet retrieves a specific State Service Application. Use this to assign the results to an object for use in other cmdlets, as shown in Listing 18.7.

LISTING 18.7 **Assigning a Variable to a Specific State Service Application**

```
$stateSA = Get-SPStateServiceApplication -Identity 5da22672-b2ad-4e68-
b725-1e91a7e693eb
```

TIP You may use the display name of the State Service Application in quotes instead of providing the GUID.

Rename a State Service Application

Scenario/Problem: You want to rename a specific State Service Application.

Solution: Use the `Set-SPStateServiceApplication` cmdlet with the `Name` parameter.

You can rename a State Service Application by using the `Set-SPStateServiceApplication` cmdlet along with the `Name` parameter. The `Identity` parameter must be used to identify the state service application that should be modified. Listing 18.8 shows an example command line.

LISTING 18.8 **Renaming a State Service Application**

```
Set-SPStateServiceApplication -Identity 5da22672-b2ad-4e68-b725-
1e91a7e693eb -Name "State Service App"
```

TIP You may use the display name of the State Service Application in quotes instead of providing the GUID. Changing the name changes the display name so the new name will become the new identity alternative.

Perform State Service Database Operations

Scenario/Problem: You need to perform various database operations on the underlying state service databases.

Solution: Use the `SPStateServiceDatabase` cmdlets.

Many database operations can be performed on the state service databases. You can display a listing of available cmdlets by issuing the command line shown in Listing 18.9. Figure 18.3 shows the result.

LISTING 18.9 **Command Line to Display the Database Operations**

```
SPStateServiceDatabase -?
```

FIGURE 18.3 Displaying the available state service database operations.

Use any of the provided cmdlets to perform the desired database operation.

CHAPTER 19

Work Management Service

This chapter explores the administrative aspects of the Work Management Services through the use of SharePoint PowerShell cmdlets.

Get the Identity of the Work Management Service Application

> **Scenario/Problem:** You need to find the identity of the Work Management Service application.

Solution: Use the `Get-SPServiceApplication` cmdlet.

To get a specific instance of a Work Management Service application, you need the identity of the service application. No cmdlet exists for getting a Work Management Service application, so you need to use the `Get-SPServiceApplication` cmdlet to display all service applications and find the Work Management Service. Listing 19.1 shows the command line without any parameters.

LISTING 19.1 **Displaying the List of Service Applications**

```
Get-SPServiceApplication
```

Get a Specific Work Management Service Application Instance

> **Scenario/Problem:** You need to obtain a metadata service application instance reference.

Solution: Use the `Get-SPServiceApplication` cmdlet to assign a variable the results using the `-Identity` parameter.

Providing the identity of the Work Management Service Application instance with the `Get-SPServiceApplication` cmdlet retrieves a specific Work Management Service instance. Use this to assign the results to an object for use in other cmdlets, as shown in Listing 19.2.

LISTING 19.2 **Assigning a Variable to a Specific Work Management Service Application**

```
$workMgmt = Get-SPServiceApplication
-Identity 61295eb2-c947-4bab-9333-3adee98d9125
```

Instead of the GUID, you can use the display name. The default display name for the Work Management Service application is Work Management Service. Because this is a long name, when displaying the service applications, the full text is cut off.

Configure the Refresh Threshold

Scenario/Problem: You would like to configure the minimum time between provider refreshes within the Work Management Service application.

Solution: Use the Set-SPWorkManagementServiceApplication cmdlet with the -MinimumTimeBetweenProviderRefreshes parameter.

You can use the -MinimumTimeBetweenProviderRefreshes cmdlet to configure the minimum amount of time between cache updates. This is on a per-user basis. The service application waits until the time specified before it processes new refresh requests.

The data type of this parameter is System.TimeSpan; therefore, creating a new time span variable to provide is recommended (see Listing 19.3).

LISTING 19.3 **Configuring the Refresh Setting**

```
$refreshTimeSpan = New-TimeSpan -Minutes 15
Set-SPWorkManagementServiceApplication
-Identity "Work Management Service"
-MinimumTimeBetweenProviderRefreshes $refreshTimeSpan
```

The Identity parameter also can be a specific Work Management Service application instance using the Get-SPServiceApplication cmdlet, as explained in the previous section.

Configure the Search Query Threshold

Scenario/Problem: You would like to configure the minimum time between calls to the Search Service within the Work Management Service application.

Solution: Use the Set-SPWorkManagementServiceApplication cmdlet with the -MinimumTimeBetweenSearchQueries parameter.

You can use the -MinimumTimeBetweenSearchQueries cmdlet to configure the minimum amount of time between calls to the Search Service to identify updated or new tasks within task lists. The search query occurs during the provider refresh

process. The service application waits until the time specified before it processes new search queries.

The data type of this parameter is `System.TimeSpan`; therefore, creating a new time span variable to provide is recommended (see Listing 19.4).

LISTING 19.4 **Configuring the Search Query Setting**

```
$refreshTimeSpan = New-TimeSpan -Minutes 15
Set-SPWorkManagementServiceApplication
-Identity "Work Management Service"
-MinimumTimeBetweenSearchQueries $refreshTimeSpan
```

The `Identity` parameter also can be a specific Work Management Service application instance using the `Get-SPServiceApplication` cmdlet, as explained in the previous section.

Configure the User Synchronization Per Server

Scenario/Problem: You would like to configure the maximum number of users that each server can synchronize.

Solution: Use the `Set-SPWorkManagementServiceApplication` cmdlet with the `-NumberOfExchangeJobsPerServer` parameter.

You can use the `-NumberOfExchangeJobsPerServer` cmdlet to configure the maximum number of users that may be synchronized per server. A server is categorized by any server in the farm that is running the Exchange Server sync timer job.

The data type for this parameter is `System.UInt32`; therefore, you may provide an integer value, as shown in Listing 19.5. The minimum value technically should be the number of SharePoint users divided by the number of servers that run timer jobs.

LISTING 19.5 **Configuring the User Synchronization Setting**

```
Set-SPWorkManagementServiceApplication
-Identity "Work Management Service"
-NumberOfExchangeJobsPerServer 1000
```

The actual timer job is named Work Management Synchronize with Exchange.

Get the Identity of the Work Management Service Application Proxy

Scenario/Problem: You need to find the identity of the Metadata Service Proxy.

Solution: Use the `Get-SPServiceApplicationProxy` cmdlet.

To get a specific instance of a Work Management Service Application Proxy, you need the identity of the Service Application Proxy. No specific cmdlet exists to get the proxy of a Work Management Service application, so you need to use the `Get-SPServiceApplicationProxy` cmdlet to display all service application proxies and find the Work Management Service. Listing 19.6 shows the command line without any parameters.

LISTING 19.6 **Displaying the List of Service Application Proxies**

```
Get-SPServiceApplicationProxy
```

NOTE Even though the list of proxies looks identical to the service applications, the GUIDs are different. You need to know the Metadata Service Proxy for certain configuration operations described in this chapter.

Get a Specific Work Management Service Application Proxy Instance

Scenario/Problem: You need to obtain a Metadata Service Application Proxy instance reference.

Solution: Use the `Get-SPWorkManagementServiceApplicationProxy` cmdlet to assign a variable the results using the `-Identity` parameter.

Providing the identity of the proxy with the `Get-SPWorkManagementService ApplicationProxy` cmdlet retrieves a specific Work Management Service Application Proxy instance. Use this to assign the results to an object for use in other cmdlets, as shown in Listing 19.7.

LISTING 19.7 **Assigning a Variable to a Specific Work Management Service Proxy**

```
$workMgmtProxy = Get-SPServiceApplicationProxy -Identity f1e2d3bb-
904b-470c-8061-d28e6f411fd7
```

Instead of the GUID, you can use the display name. The default display name for the Work Management Service application proxy is Work Management Service. Because this is a long name, when displaying the service application proxies, the full text is cut off.

CHAPTER 20

Machine Translation Service

This chapter explores the administrative aspects of Machine Translation Services through the use of SharePoint PowerShell cmdlets.

Get the Identity of the Machine Translation Service Application

Scenario/Problem: You need to find the identity of the Machine Translation Service application.

Solution: Use the Get-SPServiceApplication cmdlet.

To get a specific instance of a Machine Translation Service application, you need the identity of the service application. No cmdlet exists for getting a Machine Translation Service application, so you need to use the Get-SPServiceApplication cmdlet to display all service applications and find the Machine Translation Service. Listing 20.1 shows the command line without any parameters.

LISTING 20.1 **Displaying the List of Service Applications**

```
Get-SPServiceApplication
```

Get a Specific Machine Translation Service Application Instance

Scenario/Problem: You need to obtain a Machine Translation Service application instance reference.

Solution: Use the Get-SPServiceApplication cmdlet to assign a variable the results using the -Identity parameter.

Providing the identity of the Machine Translation Service Application instance with the Get-SPServiceApplication cmdlet retrieves a specific Machine Translation Service instance. Use this to assign the results to an object for use in other cmdlets, as shown in Listing 20.2.

LISTING 20.2 **Assigning a Variable to a Specific Machine Translation Service Application**

```
$translation = Get-SPServiceApplication
-Identity 9e5136d3-c1ff-4ef4-b5cd-8fa6c07f027a
```

Instead of the GUID, you can use the display name. The default display name for the managed Machine Translation Service application is `Machine Translation Service`. Because this is a long name, when displaying the service applications, the full text is cut off.

Get the Identity of the Machine Translation Service Proxy

Scenario/Problem: You need to find the identity of the Machine Translation Service Proxy.

Solution: Use the `Get-SPServiceApplicationProxy` cmdlet.

To get a specific instance of a Machine Translation Service Application Proxy, you need the identity of the service application proxy. No specific cmdlet exists for getting the proxy of a Machine Translation Service application, so you need to use the `Get-SPServiceApplicationProxy` cmdlet to display all service application proxies and find the Machine Translation Service. Listing 20.3 shows the command line without any parameters.

LISTING 20.3 **Displaying the List of Service Application Proxies**

```
Get-SPServiceApplicationProxy
```

NOTE Even though the list of proxies looks identical to the service applications, the GUIDs are different. You need to know the metadata service proxy for certain configuration operations described in this chapter.

Get a Specific Machine Translation Service Application Proxy Instance

Scenario/Problem: You need to obtain a metadata service application proxy instance reference.

Solution: Use the `SPServiceApplicationProxy` cmdlet to assign a variable the results using the `-Identity` parameter.

Providing the identity of the proxy with the `SPServiceApplicationProxy` cmdlet retrieves a specific Machine Translation Service Application Proxy instance. Use this to assign the results to an object for use in other cmdlets, as shown in Listing 20.4.

LISTING 20.4 **Assigning a Variable to a Specific Machine Translation Service Proxy**

```
$workMgmtProxy = Get-SPServiceApplicationProxy -Identity f1e2d3bb-904b-470c-8061-d28e6f411fd7
```

Instead of the GUID, you can use the display name. The default display name for the managed Machine Translation Service application proxy is `Machine Translation Service`. Because this is a long name, when displaying the service application proxies, the full text is cut off.

Configure the Translation Processes

Scenario/Problem: You need to modify the number of conversion processes on each server running Translation Services.

Solution: Use the `TotalActiveProcesses` parameter with the `Set-SPTranslationServiceApplication` cmdlet.

The `TotalActiveProcesses` parameter determines the how many active translation processes can occur on each server running the Word Services service application. The default is only one process. The valid entries range from 1 to 5, with the default being 1. Listing 20.5 shows a sample modification of the active translation processes.

LISTING 20.5 **Setting the Total Active Translation Processes**

```
Set-SPTranslationServiceApplication
-Identity "Translation Services" -TotalActiveProcesses 5
```

TIP The default identity of the Machine Translation Service application is "Translation Services." To find the correct name or GUID, use `Get-SPServiceApplication`.

Configure Translations Throughput

Scenario/Problem: You need to configure the throughput for the Machine Translation Services translations.

Solution: Use the `TimerJobFrequency` and `TranslationsPerInstance` parameters with the `Set-SPTranslationServiceApplication` cmdlet.

The translation throughput parameters `TimerJobFrequency` and `TranslationsPerInstance` correspond to the Machine Translation Services configuration settings, as shown in Figure 20.1.

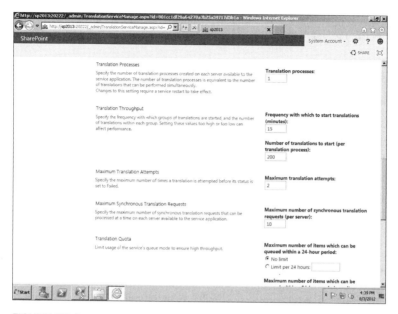

FIGURE 20.1 Translation throughput configuration settings in Central Administration.

TIP To get to these properties, from Central Administration, click on the Manage Service Applications link under Application Management. Locate the Machine Translation Services entry and highlight the connection and then click on the Properties button from the top ribbon bar.

The `TimerJobFrequency` parameter determines how often the translation process should be started using the corresponding service timer job. The default is 15 minutes, and the valid range may be any number of minutes between 1 and 59.

The `TranslationsPerInstance` parameter determines how many translations can be processed per instance. The default value is 300 translations.

Listing 20.6 shows a sample command line for setting the translation throughput values.

LISTING 20.6 Setting the Translation Throughput Values

```
Set-SPTranslationServiceApplication
-Identity "Machine Translation Services"
-TimerJobFrequency 5 -TranslationsPerInstance 100
```

The values for throughput should be modified based on usage of Machine Translation Services within your organization. Heavy usage might warrant more frequent timer job execution. Increasing the number of minutes for the timer job might warrant an increase in translations per instance; however, increasing these values could cause performance issues. Use these values along with the active processes to balance the usage and optimize throughput.

Configure Enabled Document File Extensions for Translation

Scenario/Problem: You need to modify the enabled document formats for Machine Translation Services.

Solution: Use the `AddEnabledFileExtensions` and `RemoveEnabledFile Extensions` parameters with the `Set-SPTranslationServiceApplication` cmdlet.

By default, all available document file extensions are supported within Machine Translation Services. You can use the `AddEnabledFileExtensions` or `RemoveEnabledFileExtensions` parameter with the `Set-SPTranslationServiceApplication` cmdlet to modify which set of file extensions is enabled.

Both of these parameters take a comma-separated list of valid document file extensions. The recognized values are as follows:

- docx
- doc
- docm
- dotx
- dotm
- dot
- rtf

- html
- htm
- aspx
- xhtml
- xhtm
- txt
- xlf

These file extensions correspond to the options available through Central Administration, as shown in Figure 20.2. Listing 20.7 shows sample command lines.

LISTING 20.7 **Modifying the Enabled File Extensions**

```
Set-SPTranslationServiceApplication
-Identity "Machine Translation Services" -RemoveEnabledFileExtensions
rtf,mht
```

```
Set-SPTranslationServiceApplication
-Identity "Machine Translation Services" -AddEnabledFileExtensions
docx,doc
```

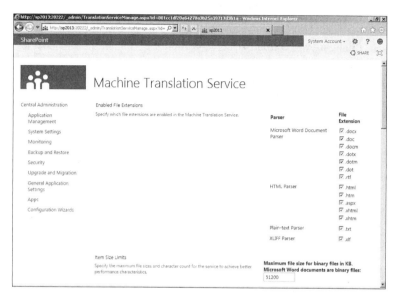

FIGURE 20.2 Supported document extensions for Machine Translation Services.

TIP When scripting out supported file format operations, use the
`ClearEnabledFileExtensions` parameter first to start with a clean slate; then just
add the supported types. This ensures that any unsupported types do not remain
active.

You can use quotation marks around a single file format; however, when you are
providing a comma-separated list of file extensions, you cannot use quotation marks.
No errors will be presented, but the operation will not modify the settings.

Modify Database Information

Scenario/Problem: You need to modify the database that Word Services
should use.

Solution: Use the database parameters with the `Set-SPTranslationService`
`Application` cmdlet.

Three database parameters can be used to configure the database settings for Word Services: DatabaseServer, DatabaseName, and DatabaseCredential. The DatabaseCredential parameter is used only if the authorization is performed through SQL authentication. Even though all these parameters are optional overall, if the DatabaseCredential parameter is used, then DatabaseServer and DatabaseName become required. Listing 20.8 shows a sample modification of the database settings.

LISTING 20.8 **Changing the Database Configuration for Translation Services**

```
$trans = Get-SPServiceApplication
-Identity 9e5136d3-c1ff-4ef4-b5cd-8fa6c07f027a
Set-SPTranslationServiceApplication -Identity $trans
-DatabaseServer SP2013 -DatabaseCredential (Get-Credential)
```

> **TIP** Use inline credentials instead of (Get-Credential). See Chapter 2, "PowerShell Basics," for more details.

If the database that is described within the DatabaseName parameter does not exist, it is created automatically.

> **TIP** Use the database parameters to create a new database without the GUID. Delete the old TranslationService_GUID database afterward.

Modify Translation Timeouts

> **Scenario/Problem:** You need to modify conversion timeout values either for running or nonresponsive conversions.

Solution: Use the KeepAliveTimeout or MaximumTranslationTime parameters with the Set-SPTranslationServiceApplication cmdlet.

To confuse matters, the MaximumTranslationTime parameter explained in the previous section deals with job monitoring, not the timeouts of translation processing. Use the KeepAliveTimeout parameter to determine how many seconds a process can be nonresponsive before it is terminated. The valid values for this setting are from 60 to 600 seconds; the default is 60 seconds.

Use the MaximumTranslationTime parameter to determine how long a translation should continue running. The default is 600 seconds, whereas the valid range is 600 to 3,600 seconds. Listing 20.9 shows a sample modification of the translation timeout setting.

LISTING 20.9 **Changing the Translation Timeout Settings**

```
Set-SPTranslationServiceApplication -Identity "Machine Translation
Services" -KeepAliveTimeout 120 -MaximumTranslationTime 1200
```

These values cannot be configured through the service application settings in Central Administration. As of this writing, they are available only via the `Set-SPTranslationServiceApplication` cmdlet.

Modify the Maximum Translation Attempts

Scenario/Problem: You need to modify the maximum conversion attempts in Word Services.

Solution: Use the `MaximumTranslationAttempts` parameter with the `Set-SPTranslationServiceApplication` cmdlet.

Use the `MaximumTranslationAttempts` parameter to configure how many attempts should be taken before a translation is considered a failure. The default is 2 (attempts), and the range of valid values is 1 to 10. Listing 20.10 shows a sample modification of the maximum translation attempts setting.

LISTING 20.10 **Changing the Maximum Translation Attempts Setting**

```
Set-SPTranslationServiceApplication
-Identity "Machine Translation Services" -MaximumTranslationAttempts 3
```

The default is two attempts, but three seems like a normal setting. Anything more than five is probably too optimistic. If the translation fails after three times, there is a 90% chance that it will continue to fail.

Modify the Recycle Threshold

Scenario/Problem: You need to modify the recycle threshold of the conversion processes in Machine Translation Services.

Solution: Use the `RecycleProcessThreshold` parameter with the `Set-SPTranslationServiceApplication` cmdlet.

The `RecycleProcessThreshold` parameter enables you to specify the number of documents each translation process can convert before the process is recycled. The default value is `100` (documents), whereas the valid range of values is `1` to `1000`. Listing 20.11 shows a sample threshold modification.

LISTING 20.11 **Changing the Recycle Threshold**

```
Set-SPTranslationServiceApplication
-Identity "Machine Translation Services" -RecycleProcessThreshold 200
```

CHAPTER 21

Excel Services

This chapter explores the administrative aspects of Excel Services through the use of SharePoint PowerShell cmdlets.

Create a Trusted File Location

Scenario/Problem: You need to create a new trusted file location for Excel Services.

Solution: Use the `New-SPExcelFileLocation` cmdlet.

The `New-SPExcelFileLocation` cmdlet can be used to create a new trusted location to access Excel workbooks. Provide the address of the location and the Excel Services Application instance, as shown in Listing 21.1.

LISTING 21.1 **Creating a New Trusted File Location**

```
New-SPExcelFileLocation -Address "http://sp2010/Excel Workbooks"
-ExcelServiceApplication "Excel Services Application"
-LocationType SharePoint -IncludeChildren
```

The `-LocationType` parameter can be one of the following:

- ▶ `SharePoint` (default)
- ▶ `UNC`
- ▶ `HTTP`

The `-IncludeChildren` switch parameter is used to specify that any folders or locations underneath the address should also be trusted.

Upon successful creation of the new trusted file location, a summary of the properties is displayed, as shown in Figure 21.1.

TIP The default Excel Services application is named "Excel Services Application." To find the correct name or GUID, use `Get-SPServiceApplication` or `Get-SPExcelServiceApplication`.

FIGURE 21.1 Creating a new trusted file location.

Display All Trusted File Locations

Scenario/Problem: You need to display all trusted file locations for an Excel Services application.

Solution: Use the `Get-SPExcelFileLocation` cmdlet with the `ExcelServiceApplication` parameter.

Using the `Get-SPExcelFileLocation` cmdlet with the `ExcelServiceApplication` parameter (see Listing 21.2) displays all configured trusted file locations, as shown in Figure 21.2.

LISTING 21.2 **Displaying All Trusted File Locations**

```
Get-SPExcelFileLocation
-ExcelServiceApplication "Excel Services Application"
```

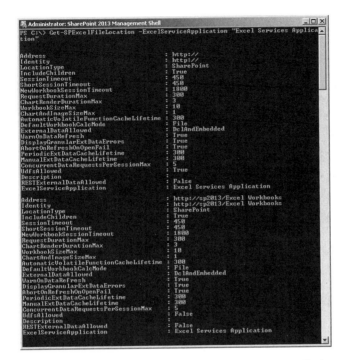

FIGURE 21.2 The `Get-SPExcelFileLocation` cmdlet displays all trusted file locations.

Get a Specific Trusted File Location

Scenario/Problem: You need to obtain a specific trusted file location reference.

Solution: Use the `Get-SPExcelFileLocation` cmdlet to assign a variable the results using the `-Identity` and `-ExcelServiceApplication` parameters.

Providing the identity of the trusted file location to the `Get-SPExcelFileLocation` cmdlet retrieves a specific trusted file location instance. Use this to assign the results to a variable for use in other cmdlets, as shown in Listing 21.3.

LISTING 21.3 **Assigning a Variable to a Specific Trusted File Location**

```
$trustedLocation = Get-SPExcelFileLocation
-Identity "http://sp2010/Excel Workbooks"
-ExcelServiceApplication "Excel Services Application"
```

> **TIP** When you are creating a new trusted file location, the `Address` becomes the same as the `Identity` property, as shown in the results. Refer to the figures in the previous sections for examples.

Remove a Trusted File Location

> **Scenario/Problem:** You need to remove a trusted file location from Excel Services.

Solution: Use the `Remove-SPExcelFileLocation` cmdlet with a trusted file location variable.

The `Remove-SPExcelFileLocation` cmdlet enables you to remove a specific trusted file location from Excel Services. Use this in conjunction with the `Get-SPExcelFileLocation` cmdlet (explained in a previous section), as shown in Listing 21.4.

LISTING 21.4 **Sample Script for Removing a Trusted File Location**

```
$trustedLocation = Get-SPExcelFileLocation -Identity "http://sp2010/Excel
Workbooks" -ExcelServiceApplication "Excel Services Application"
Remove-SPExcelFileLocation $trustedLocation
-ExcelServiceApplication "Excel Service Application"
```

> **NOTE** Even though the `$trustedLocation` object variable contains the Excel Service Application property, the `–ExcelServiceApplication` parameter is still required. For simplification, you may use the file location identity instead of the variable.

Create a Trusted Data Connection Library

> **Scenario/Problem:** You need to create a new trusted data connection library for Excel Services.

Solution: Use the `New-SPExcelDataConnectionLibrary` cmdlet.

The `New-SPExcelDataConnectionLibrary` cmdlet can be used to create a new trusted data connection location that Excel workbooks can access. Provide the address of the data connection library and the Excel Services Application instance, as shown in Listing 21.5.

LISTING 21.5 **Creating a New Trusted Data Connection Library**

```
New-SPExcelDataConnectionLibrary
-Address "http://sp2010/Data Connections"
-ExcelServiceApplication "Excel Services Application"
```

Upon successful creation of the new trusted data connection library, a summary of the properties is displayed, as shown in Figure 21.3.

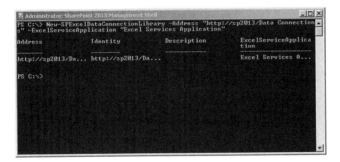

FIGURE 21.3 Creating a new data connection library entry.

Display All Trusted Data Connection Libraries

Scenario/Problem: You need to display all trusted data connection libraries configured for an Excel Services application.

Solution: Use the `Get-SPExcelDataConnectionLibrary` cmdlet with the `ExcelServiceApplication` parameter.

Using the `Get-SPExcelDataConnectionLibrary` cmdlet with the `ExcelServiceApplication` parameter, as shown in Listing 21.6, displays all configured trusted data connection libraries.

LISTING 21.6 **Displaying All Trusted Data Connection Libraries**

```
Get-SPExcelDataConnectionLibrary
-ExcelServiceApplication "Excel Services Application"
```

Get a Specific Trusted Data Connection Library

Scenario/Problem: You need to obtain a specific trusted data connection library reference.

Solution: Use the `Get-SPExcelDataConnectionLibrary` cmdlet to assign a variable the results using the `-Identity` and `-ExcelServiceApplication` parameters.

Providing the identity of the trusted data connection library to the `Get-SPExcelDataConnectionLibrary` cmdlet retrieves a specific data connection library instance. Use this to assign the results to a variable for use in other cmdlets, as shown in Listing 21.7.

LISTING 21.7 **Assigning a Variable to a Specific Data Connection Library**

```
$trustedLibrary = Get-SPExcelDataConnectionLibrary
-Identity "http://sp2010/Data Connections"
-ExcelServiceApplication "Excel Services Application"
```

TIP When you are creating a new trusted file location, the `Identity` becomes the same value as the `Address` property, as shown in the results. Refer to the figures in the previous sections for examples.

Remove a Trusted Data Connection Library

Scenario/Problem: You need to remove a trusted data connection library from Excel Services.

Solution: Use the `Remove-SPExcelDataConnectionLibrary` cmdlet with a trusted data connection library variable.

The `Remove-SPExcelDataConnectionLibrary` cmdlet enables you to remove a specific trusted data connection library from Excel Services. Use this in conjunction with the `Get-SPExcelDataConnectionLibrary` cmdlet (explained in a previous section), as shown in Listing 21.8.

LISTING 21.8 **Sample Script for Removing a Trusted Data Connection Library**

```
$trustedLibrary = Get-SPExcelDataConnectionLibrary
-Identity "http://sp2010/Data Connections"
-ExcelServiceApplication "Excel Services Application"
Remove-SPExcelDataConnectionLibrary $trustedLibrary
-ExcelServiceApplication "Excel Service Application"
```

NOTE For simplification, you may use the file location identity instead of the `$trustedLibrary` variable.

Create a New Safe Data Provider

Scenario/Problem: You need to create a new safe data provider for Excel Services.

Solution: Use the `New-SPExcelDataProvider` cmdlet.

The `New-SPExcelDataProvider` cmdlet can be used to create a new safe data provider that Excel workbooks can access via a data connection. Provide the provider information and the Excel Services Application instance, as shown in Listing 21.9.

LISTING 21.9 **Creating a New Safe Data Provider**

```
New-SPExcelDataProvider
-ExcelServiceApplication "Excel Services Application"
-ProviderID "Custom DB" -ProviderType ODBC
```

The `-ProviderID` is an identifier for the data provider. The `-ProviderType` can be any of the following values:

- OLEDB
- ODBC
- ODBCDSN

TIP Verify third-party data provider documentation for the proper provider ID and provider type to use.

Upon successful creation of the new safe data provider, a summary of the properties is displayed, as shown in Figure 21.4.

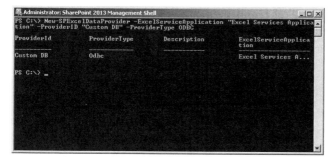

FIGURE 21.4 Creating a new data provider entry.

Display All Safe Data Providers

Scenario/Problem: You need to display all safe data providers configured for an Excel Services application.

Solution: Use the `Get-SPExcelDataProvider` cmdlet with the `ExcelServiceApplication` parameter.

Using the `Get-SPExcelDataProvider` cmdlet with the `ExcelServiceApplication` parameter, as shown in Listing 21.10, displays all configured trusted data connection libraries.

LISTING 21.10 **Displaying All Safe Data Providers**

```
Get-SPExcelDataProvider
-ExcelServiceApplication "Excel Services Application"
```

Get a Specific Safe Data Provider

Scenario/Problem: You need to obtain a specific safe data provider reference.

Solution: Use the `Get-SPExcelDataProvider` cmdlet with a piped `where` clause.

The `Get-SPExcelDataProvider` cmdlet does not have an `Identity` or `ProviderID` parameter; therefore, it returns only the entire list of safe data providers. Therefore, you need to pipe the output to a `where` clause that finds the particular data provider based on the provider ID. To accomplish this filtering while providing the required Excel

Service Application object, you first need to pipe the Excel Service Application object into the `Get-SPExcelDataProvider` cmdlet.

This sounds more complicated than it actually is implemented. Listing 21.11 shows an example.

LISTING 21.11 **Assigning a Variable to a Specific Data Provider**

```
$dataProvider = Get-SPExcelServiceApplication
-Identity "Excel Services Application" | Get-SPExcelDataProvider
 | where {$_.ProviderID -eq "Custom DB"}
```

Remove a Safe Data Provider

Scenario/Problem: You need to remove a safe data provider from Excel Services.

Solution: Use the `Remove-SPExcelDataProvider` cmdlet with a safe data provider variable.

The `Remove-SPExcelDataProvider` cmdlet enables you to remove a specific safe data provider from Excel Services. Use this in conjunction with the `Get-SPExcelDataProvider` cmdlet (explained in a previous section), as shown in Listing 21.12.

LISTING 21.12 **Sample Script for Removing a Safe Data Provider**

```
$dataProvider = Get-SPExcelServiceApplication
-Identity "Excel Services Application" | Get-SPExcelDataProvider
 | where {$_.ProviderID -eq "Custom DB"}

Remove-SPExcelDataProvider $dataProvider
```

The `Remove-SPExcelDataProvider` cmdlet doesn't require an Excel Service Application parameter, which makes up for the trouble of having to generate the proper data provider object.

Create a Blocked File Type

Scenario/Problem: You need to block a file type for Excel Services.

Solution: Use the `New-SPExcelBlockedFileType` cmdlet.

The `New-SPExcelBlockedFileType` cmdlet can be used to block a specific type of Excel workbook from Excel Services. Provide the file type and the Excel Services Application instance, as shown in Listing 21.13.

LISTING 21.13 **Creating a New Blocked File Type**

```
New-SPExcelBlockedFileType
-ExcelServiceApplication "Excel Services Application" -FileType XLSB
```

The `-FileType` can be one of the following:

- ► XLSX
- ► XLSM
- ► XLSB

Essentially, you are blocking Excel workbooks, macro-enabled workbooks, or binary-enabled workbooks (or some combination thereof).

Display All Blocked File Types

Scenario/Problem: You need to display all blocked file types for an Excel Services application.

Solution: Use the `Get-SPExcelBlockedFileType` cmdlet with the `ExcelServiceApplication` parameter.

Using the `Get-SPExcelBlockedFileType` cmdlet with the `ExcelServiceApplication` parameter, as shown in Listing 21.14, displays all configured blocked file types.

LISTING 21.14 **Displaying All Blocked File Types**

```
Get-SPExcelBlockedFileType
-ExcelServiceApplication "Excel Services Application"
```

Get a Specific Blocked File Type

Scenario/Problem: You need to obtain a specific trusted file location reference.

Solution: Use the `Get-SPExcelBlockedFileType` cmdlet to assign a variable the results using the `-Identity` and `-ExcelServiceApplication` parameters.

Providing the identity of the blocked file type to the `Get-SPExcelBlockedFileType` cmdlet retrieves a specific blocked file type instance. Use this to assign the results to a variable for use in other cmdlets, as shown in Listing 21.15.

LISTING 21.15 **Assigning a Variable to a Specific Blocked File Type**

```
$blockedFileType = Get-SPExcelBlockedFileType
-Identity "XLSB" -ExcelServiceApplication "Excel Services Application"
```

> **TIP** When you are creating a new blocked file type, the `Identity` becomes the same value as the `File Type` property.

Remove a Blocked File Type

> **Scenario/Problem:** You need to remove a trusted file location from Excel Services.

Solution: Use the `Remove-SPExcelBlockedFileType` cmdlet with a blocked file type variable.

The `Remove-SPExcelBlockedFileType` cmdlet enables you to remove a specific blocked file type from Excel Services. Use this in conjunction with the `Get-SPExcelBlockedFileType` cmdlet (explained in a previous section), as shown in Listing 21.16.

LISTING 21.16 **Sample Script for Removing a Blocked File Type**

```
$blockedFileType = Get-SPExcelBlockedFileType -Identity "XLSB"
-ExcelServiceApplication "Excel Services Application"
Remove-SPExcelBlockedFileType $blockedFileType
-ExcelServiceApplication "Excel Service Application"
```

> **NOTE** Even though the `$blockedFileType` object variable contains the Excel Service Application property, the `—ExcelServiceApplication` parameter is still required. For simplification, you may use the file type identity instead of the variable.

Create a User-Defined Function Reference

> **Scenario/Problem:** You need to configure a user-defined function reference for use in Excel Services

Solution: Use the `New-SPExcelUserDefinedFunction` cmdlet.

The `New-SPExcelUserDefinedFunction` cmdlet can be used to create a reference to an assembly that can call user-defined functions within Excel workbooks running under Excel Services. Provide the assembly information and the Excel Services Application instance, as shown in Listing 21.17.

LISTING 21.17 **Creating a New User-Defined Function Reference**

```
New-SPExcelUserDefinedFunction -ExcelServiceApplication "Excel Services
Application" -Assembly "MyCompany.ExcelServices.UDF,
Version=1.0.0.0, Culture=neutral, PublicKeyToken=82e6dce111e9429c"
-AssemblyLocation GAC
```

The `-AssemblyLocation` can be one of the following:

▶ GAC

▶ LocalFile

For security as well as central access, user-defined functions should be compiled into a DLL and placed in the GAC.

Display All User-Defined Function References

Scenario/Problem: You need to display all user-defined function references configured for an Excel Services application.

Solution: Use the `Get-SPExcelUserDefinedFunction` cmdlet with the `ExcelServiceApplication` parameter.

Using the `Get-SPExcelUserDefinedFunction` cmdlet with the `ExcelServiceApplication` parameter, as shown in Listing 21.18, displays all configured user-defined functions.

LISTING 21.18 **Displaying All User-Defined Function References**

```
Get-SPExcelUserDefinedFunction
-ExcelServiceApplication "Excel Services Application"
```

Get a Specific User-Defined Function Reference

Scenario/Problem: You need to obtain a specific user-defined function reference.

Solution: Use the `Get-SPExcelUserDefinedFunction` cmdlet to assign a variable the results using the `-Identity` and `-ExcelServiceApplication` parameters.

Providing the identity of the user-defined function to the `Get-SPExcelUserDefinedFunction` cmdlet retrieves a specific user-defined function instance. Use this to assign the results to a variable for use in other cmdlets, as shown in Listing 21.19.

LISTING 21.19 **Assigning a Variable to a Specific User-Defined Function**

```
$udfReference = Get-SPExcelUserDefinedFunction
-ExcelServiceApplication "Excel Services Application"
-Identity "Microsoft.Office.Server.WebAnalytics.UI, Version=15.0.0.0,
Culture=neutral, PublicKeyToken=71e9bce111e9429c"
```

TIP When you are creating a new user-defined function reference, the `Identity` becomes the same value as the `Assembly` property.

Remove a User-Defined Function Reference

Scenario/Problem: You need to remove a user-defined function reference from Excel Services.

Solution: Use the `Remove-SPExcelUserDefinedFunction` cmdlet with a user-defined function variable.

The `Remove-SPExcelUserDefinedFunction` cmdlet enables you to remove a specific user-defined function from Excel Services. Use this in conjunction with the `Get-SPExcelUserDefinedFunction` cmdlet (explained in a previous section), as shown in Listing 21.20.

LISTING 21.20 **Sample Script for Removing a User-Defined Function**

```
$udfReference = Get-SPExcelUserDefinedFunction
-ExcelServiceApplication "Excel Services Application"
-Identity "Microsoft.Office.Server.WebAnalytics.UI, Version=15.0.0.0,
```

```
Culture=neutral, PublicKeyToken=71e9bce111e9429c"

Remove-SPExcelUserDefinedFunction $udfReference
-ExcelServiceApplication "Excel Service Application"
```

> **NOTE** Even though the $udfReference object variable contains the Excel Service Application property, the —ExcelServiceApplication parameter is still required. For simplification, you may use the user-defined function identity instead of the variable.

Modify Excel Services Objects

> **Scenario/Problem:** You need to modify properties of various Excel Services objects.

Solution: Use the cmdlets listed in this section to change the configuration of existing trusted file locations, trusted data connection libraries, safe data providers, blocked file types, user-defined function references, and the Excel Services application itself.

This chapter covers the basic or more common cmdlets for creating and using Excel Services objects. For more advanced scripting and modifications of these objects, the following cmdlets are available:

- ▶ Set-SPExcelServiceApplication
- ▶ Set-SPExcelDataConnectionLibrary
- ▶ Set-SPExcelDataProvider
- ▶ Set-SPExcelFileLocation
- ▶ Set-SPExcelUserDefinedFunction

CHAPTER 22

PerformancePoint Services

This chapter explores the administrative aspects of PerformancePoint Services through the use of SharePoint PowerShell cmdlets. These are probably the longest cmdlets for SharePoint and do behave differently when compared to other service applications such as Excel Services.

Configure the Unattended Service Account

Scenario/Problem: You need to configure the unattended account for PerformancePoint Services

Solution: Use the `Set-SPPerformancePointSecureDataValues` cmdlet.

One of the first things you need to do to use PerformancePoint Services (PPS) within SharePoint 2013 is set the unattended service account. This account is used to access the data sources for PPS. This can be easily facilitated using the `Set-SPPerformancePointSecureDataValues` cmdlet, as shown in Listing 22.1.

LISTING 22.1 **Setting the Unattended Service Account**

```
Set-SPPerformancePointSecureDataValues    -ServiceApplication
"PerformancePoint Service Application"
-DataSourceUnattendedServiceAccount (Get-Credential)
```

The default PerformancePoint Services Application is named PerformancePoint Service Application. To find the correct name or GUID, use `Get-SPServiceApplication` or `Get-SPPerformancePointServiceApplication`.

TIP Use inline credentials instead of `(Get-Credential)`. See Chapter 2 for more details.

Display the Unattended Service Account

Scenario/Problem: You need to see which account is configured as the unattended service account.

Solution: Use the `Get-SPPerformancePointSecureDataValues` cmdlet.

To review the unattended service account that is configured for PPS data sources, use the `Get-SPPerformancePointSecureValues` cmdlet with the `-ServiceApplication` parameter, as shown in Listing 22.2.

LISTING 22.2 **Displaying the Unattended Service Account**

```
Get-SPPerformancePointSecureDataValues -ServiceApplication
"PerformancePoint Service Application"
```

The account name is displayed, but the password is not. The default
PerformancePoint Services Application is named PerformancePoint Service
Application. To find the correct name or GUID, use `Get-SPServiceApplication` or
`Get-SPPerformancePointServiceApplication`.

Create a Trusted Content Location

Scenario/Problem: You need to create a new trusted content location for
PerformancePoint Services.

Solution: Use the `New-SPPerformancePointServiceApplicationTrustedLocation`
cmdlet.

The `New-SPPerformancePointServiceApplicationTrustedLocation` is used to
create a new trusted content location to access PPS content. Provide the address (URL)
of the location, the type, and the PerformancePoint Services Application instance, as
shown in Listing 22.3.

LISTING 22.3 **Create a New Trusted Content Location**

```
New-SPPerformancePointServiceApplicationTrustedLocation -Url
"http://sp2013/Lists/PPS Content" -ServiceApplication
"PerformancePoint Service Application" -Type List -TrustedLocationType
Content
```

The `-Type` can be one of the following when creating a content location:

- ▶ `SiteCollection`
- ▶ `Site`
- ▶ `List`

Passing in `Content` with the `-TrustedLocationType` parameter determines that this
location is a content location for PPS. Although `DocumentLibrary` is a valid `-Type`, it
is not valid for content locations.

Create a Trusted Data Source Location

Scenario/Problem: You need to create a new trusted data source location for PerformancePoint Services.

Solution: Use the `New-SPPerformancePointServiceApplicationTrustedLocation` cmdlet.

The `New-SPPerformancePointServiceApplicationTrustedLocation` can be used to create a new trusted data source location so that PPS can access data connections. Provide the address (URL) of the location, the type, and the PerformancePoint Services Application instance, as shown in Listing 22.4.

LISTING 22.4 **Create a New Trusted Data Source Location**

```
New-SPPerformancePointServiceApplicationTrustedLocation -Url
"http://sp2013/PPS DataSource" -ServiceApplication "PerformancePoint
Service Application" -Type DocumentLibrary -TrustedLocationType
DataSource
```

The `-Type` can be one of the following when creating a content location:

- ▶ `SiteCollection`
- ▶ `Site`
- ▶ `DocumentLibrary`

Passing in `DataSource` with the `-TrustedLocationType` parameter determines that this location is a data source location for PPS. Although `List` is a valid `-Type`, it is not valid for data source locations.

Display All Trusted Content Locations

Scenario/Problem: You need to display all trusted content locations configured for a PerformancePoint Services Application.

Solution: Use the `Get-SPPerformancePointServiceApplicationTrustedLocation` cmdlet with a piped `where` clause.

To filter the list of trusted locations, you need to use a piped `where` clause with the `Get-SPPerformancePointServiceApplicationTrustedLocation` cmdlet. Because this cmdlet doesn't show detailed information by default, the `-Identity` parameter

must be used. The service application is therefore piped into this cmdlet. Listing 22.5 shows an example command line.

LISTING 22.5 **Display All Trusted Content Locations**

```
Get-SPPerformancePointServiceApplication "Performance Point Service
Application" | Get-SPPerformancePointServiceApplicationTrustedLocation
-Identity $_.ID | where {$_.FileType -eq "Content"}
```

Display All Trusted DataSource Locations

Scenario/Problem: You need to display all trusted data source locations configured for a PerformancePoint Services Application.

Solution: Use the `Get-SPPerformancePointServiceApplicationTrustedLocation` cmdlet with a piped `where` clause.

To filter the list of trusted locations, you need to use a piped `where` clause with the `Get-SPPerformancePointServiceApplicationTrustedLocation` cmdlet. Because this cmdlet doesn't show detailed information by default, the `-Identity` parameter must be used. The service application is therefore piped into this cmdlet. Listing 22.6 shows an example command line.

LISTING 22.6 **Display All Trusted DataSource Locations**

```
Get-SPPerformancePointServiceApplication "Performance Point Service
Application" | Get-SPPerformancePointServiceApplicationTrustedLocation
-Identity $_.ID | where {$_.FileType -eq "DataSource"}
```

Display Details of Trusted Locations

Scenario/Problem: You need to display the underlying details and identities of trusted locations.

Solution: Use the `Get-SPPerformancePointServiceApplicationTrustedLocation` cmdlet with the `-Identity` parameter piped to a `select *`.

To view all the details of the trusted locations, such as the identity GUID, you need to use the `-Identity` parameter with `Get-SPPerformancePointServiceApplication` while piping the results to a `select *` directive. The service application needs to be

piped into the `Get-SPPerformancePointServiceApplication` cmdlet, as shown in Listing 22.7.

LISTING 22.7 **Display All Details of the Trusted Locations**

```
Get-SPPerformancePointServiceApplication "Performance Point Service
Application" | Get-SPPerformancePointServiceApplicationTrustedLocation
-Identity $_.ID | select *
```

When the details are displayed, you can fine-tune your `select` directive to only retrieve the information you need (such as `select url` or `id`).

Get a Specific Trusted Location

Scenario/Problem: You need to obtain a specific trusted location reference.

Solution: Use the `Get-SPPerformancePointServiceApplicationTrustedLocation` cmdlet to assign a variable the results using the `-Identity` and `-ServiceApplication` parameters.

Providing the identity of the trusted data connection library to the `Get-SPPerformancePointServiceApplicationTrustedLocation` cmdlet retrieves a specific data connection library instance. Use this to assign the results to a variable for use in other cmdlets, as shown in Listing 22.8.

LISTING 22.8 **Assigning a Variable to a Specific Trusted Location**

```
$trustedLocation = Get-
SPPerformancePointServiceApplicationTrustedLocation -Identity
fab6396b-5cd3-4f17-be60-57ae7d18c8a6
```

Remove a Trusted Location

Scenario/Problem: You need to remove a trusted location from PerformancePoint Services.

Solution: Use the `Remove-SPPerformancePointServiceApplicationTrusted Location` cmdlet with a trusted data location variable.

The `Remove-SPPerformancePointServiceApplicationTrustedLocation` cmdlet enables you to remove a specific trusted location from PerformancePoint Services. Use

this in conjunction with the `Get-SPPerformancePointServiceApplicationTrusted` `Location` cmdlet (explained in the previous section), as shown in Listing 22.9.

LISTING 22.9 **Example Script for Removing a Trusted Location**

```
$trustedLocation = Get-
SPPerformancePointServiceApplicationTrustedLocation -Identity
fab6396b-5cd3-4f17-be60-57ae7d18c8a6
Remove-SPPerformancePointServiceApplicationTrustedLocation
$trustedLocation
```

NOTE For simplification, you may use the trusted location identity instead of the $trustedLocation variable.

Configure PerformancePoint Services to Enforce Trusted Locations

Scenario/Problem: You need to modify the PerformancePoint Service Application to use the added trusted locations.

Solution: Use the `Set-SPPerformancePointServiceApplication` cmdlet with the trusted location parameters.

By default, all SharePoint locations are trusted for content and data sources. Even if you add new locations using the cmdlets in the previous sections, they are added but not enforced.

To restrict PerformancePoint Services to use only the configured trusted locations, use the `Set-SPPerformancePointServiceApplication` cmdlet with the trusted location parameters, as shown in Listing 22.10 and Listing 22.11.

LISTING 22.10 **Enforce Trusted Content Locations**

```
Set-SPPerformancePointServiceApplication -Identity "PerformancePoint
Service Application" -TrustedContentLocationsRestricted $true
```

LISTING 22.11 **Enforce Trusted Data Source Locations**

```
Set-SPPerformancePointServiceApplication -Identity "PerformancePoint
Service Application" -TrustedDataSourceLocationsRestricted $true
```

Use `$false` to disable the enforcement of the trusted locations and allow all SharePoint locations to be acceptable.

Configure PerformancePoint Services Application Settings

> **Scenario/Problem:** You need to modify the PerformancePoint Service Application settings.

Solution: Use the `Set-SPPerformancePointServiceApplication` cmdlet with the desired parameters.

The `Set-SPPerformancePointServiceApplication` cmdlet enables you to configure various settings within the PerformancePoint Service Application specified. Pass in the name or the ID of the service application instance using the `-Identity` parameter, and use one or more of the optional parameters to modify the appropriate settings. Listing 22.12 shows an example modification of the PerformancePoint Service Application settings.

LISTING 22.12 **Modifying the PerformancePoint Service Application Settings**

```
Set-SPPerformancePointServiceApplication -Identity "PerformancePoint
Service Application" -CommentsDisabled $false -CommentsScorecardMax
100
```

CHAPTER 23

Access Services

IN THIS CHAPTER

- ▶ Configure the Application Log Size
- ▶ Configure the Cache Timeout
- ▶ Modify the Maximum Columns in a Query
- ▶ Modify the Maximum Calculated Columns in a Query
- ▶ Configure the Maximum Order By Clauses
- ▶ Configure the Maximum Number of Rows in a Query
- ▶ Configure the Maximum Number of Records in an Access Table
- ▶ Configure the Maximum Number of Sources in a Query
- ▶ Enable and Disable the Use of Outer Joins
- ▶ Allow or Restrict Nonremotable Queries
- ▶ Throttle Access Services Memory Utilization
- ▶ Throttle Session Memory Utilization
- ▶ Configure User Sessions
- ▶ Limit Template Sizes
- ▶ Modify Access Services Databases

This chapter explores the administrative aspects of Access Services through the use of SharePoint PowerShell cmdlets. Access Services is pretty light in regard to its associated PowerShell commands. Essentially, only one cmdlet is used often to configure Access Services settings. However, because many options can be configured separately, this chapter describes the scenarios for those settings. SharePoint 2013 introduces some additional database-related cmdlets for Access Services.

Configure the Application Log Size

Scenario/Problem: You need to modify the application log size for Access Services.

Solution: Use the `ApplicationLogSize` parameter with the `Set-SPAccessService Application` cmdlet.

The `ApplicationLogSize` parameter determines the maximum number of records that Access Services should log. A `-1` entry means unlimited, and `0` means none. The maximum entry is the maximum integer size (which varies by environment). The default is 3,000 records. Listing 23.1 shows a sample modification of the application log size.

LISTING 23.1 **Setting the Application Log Size**

```
Set-SPAccessServiceApplication -Identity "Access Services"
-ApplicationLogSize 5000
```

TIP The default identity of the Access Service application is "Access Services." To find the correct name or GUID, use `Get-SPServiceApplication` or `Get-SPAccessServiceApplication`.

Configure the Cache Timeout

Scenario/Problem: You need to modify the cache timeout value for Access Services.

Solution: Use the `CacheTimeout` parameter with the `Set-SPAccessServiceApplication` cmdlet.

The `CacheTimeout` parameter determines the maximum number of seconds that Access Services should cache data without user activity. A `-1` entry means never time

out. The valid range otherwise is 1 to 2073600 (that is, 2,073,600 seconds, equating to 24 days). The default is 300 seconds (5 minutes). Listing 23.2 shows a sample modification of the cache timeout.

LISTING 23.2 **Setting the Cache Timeout to 10 Minutes**

```
Set-SPAccessServiceApplication -Identity "Access Services"
-CacheTimeout 600
```

Modify the Maximum Columns in a Query

Scenario/Problem: You need to modify the maximum amount of columns in a query.

Solution: Use the `ColumnsMax` parameter with the `Set-SPAccessService Application` cmdlet.

The `ColumnsMax` parameter has a default value of 40 and determines the maximum number of columns that can participate in a query and/or be contained in the output of a query. The valid range of values for this parameter is 1 to 255. Listing 23.3 shows a sample modification of the maximum number of columns.

LISTING 23.3 **Changing the Maximum Number of Columns**

```
Set-SPAccessServiceApplication -Identity "Access Services"
-ColumnsMax 20
```

Although you might need this to increase the number of columns allowed, queries typically perform better when there are fewer columns. If possible, attempt to reduce the number of columns needed in your Access Services queries.

Modify the Maximum Calculated Columns in a Query

Scenario/Problem: You need to modify the maximum amount of calculated columns in a query.

Solution: Use the `OutputCalculatedColumnsMax` parameter with the `Set-SPAccessServiceApplication` cmdlet.

The `OutputCalculatedColumnsMax` parameter has a default value of 10 and determines the maximum number of calculated columns that can be contained in the

output of a query. This value does not include any calculated columns that are part of SharePoint lists. The valid range of values for this parameter is 0 to 32. Listing 23.4 shows a sample modification of the maximum number of calculated columns.

LISTING 23.4 **Changing the Maximum Number of Columns**

```
Set-SPAccessServiceApplication -Identity "Access Services"
-OutputCalculatedColumnsMax 5
```

> **TIP** Calculated columns may improve performance because values are precalculated and then cached. However, having many calculated columns with dynamic data may present performance issues and/or stale data.

Configure the Maximum Order By Clauses

> **Scenario/Problem:** You need to modify the maximum amount of Order By clauses in a query.

Solution: Use the OrderByMax parameter with the Set-SPAccessService Application cmdlet.

The OrderByMax parameter has a default value of 4 and determines the maximum number of Order By clauses that can be contained within a query. The valid range of values for this parameter is 0 to 8. Listing 23.5 shows a sample modification of the maximum number of Order By clauses.

LISTING 23.5 **Changing the Maximum Number of Order By Clauses**

```
Set-SPAccessServiceApplication -Identity "Access Services"
-OrderByMax 2
```

Order By clauses instantiate sorting algorithms within the query engine. Although this can be optimized with indexes, multiple Order By clauses could place a strain on the query performance. Typically, you need only one Order By to sort the results of your query; however, complex queries might require more than one.

Configure the Maximum Number of Rows in a Query

> **Scenario/Problem:** You need to modify the maximum amount of rows in a query.

Solution: Use the RowsMax parameter with the Set-SPAccessServiceApplication cmdlet.

The RowsMax parameter has a default value of 25000 and determines the maximum number of rows a list that participates in a query can contain and/or the maximum number of rows that can be contained in the results of the query. The valid range of values for this parameter is 1 to 200000. Listing 23.6 shows a sample modification of the maximum number of rows.

LISTING 23.6 **Changing the Maximum Number of Rows**

```
Set-SPAccessServiceApplication -Identity "Access Services"
-RowsMax 10000
```

Although lists and libraries have been optimized in SharePoint 2013 to allow an "unlimited" number of items, if you need to deal with entities that contain thousands of rows, you might want to consider migrating the list to an Access table or migrating the entire set of entities to a full-fledged RDBMS such as SQL Server.

Configure the Maximum Number of Records in an Access Table

Scenario/Problem: You need to modify the maximum amount of records allowed in an Access table.

Solution: Use the RecordsInTableMax parameter with the Set-SPAccessService Application cmdlet.

The RecordsInTableMax parameter has a default value of 500000 and determines the maximum number of records that can be contained within an Access table used within Access Services. An entry of -1 means unlimited, whereas the valid range of values for this parameter is 1 to the maximum integer value allowed. Listing 23.7 shows a sample modification of the maximum number of records.

LISTING 23.7 **Changing the Maximum Number of Records in a Table**

```
Set-SPAccessServiceApplication -Identity "Access Services"
-RecordsInTableMax 100000
```

If you need to manage tens of thousands of records within Access tables, you might want to consider migrating the database to a full-fledged RDBMS such as SQL Server.

Configure the Maximum Number of Sources in a Query

Scenario/Problem: You need to modify the maximum number of sources allowed in a query within Access Services.

Solution: Use the `SourcesMax` parameter with the `Set-SPAccessService Application` cmdlet.

The `SourcesMax` parameter has a default value of `12` and determines the maximum number of lists that can be used in a query within Access Services. The valid range of values for this parameter is `1` to `20`. Listing 23.8 shows a sample modification of the maximum number of sources.

LISTING 23.8 **Changing the Maximum Number of Sources in a Query**

```
Set-SPAccessServiceApplication -Identity "Access Services"
-SourcesMax 8
```

Many lists used within a query could affect performance. Limiting the number of lists is a good idea. If you need to use many lists, you might want to reevaluate the list structures or query.

Enable and Disable the Use of Outer Joins

Scenario/Problem: You need to enable or disable the use of outer joins within queries.

Solution: Use the `OuterJoinsAllowed` switch parameter with the `Set-SPAccessServiceApplication` cmdlet.

By default, the Access Services service application is configured to allow outer joins within queries. Because `OuterJoinsAllowed` is a switch parameter, you can use it with a `$false` setting to disable outer joins, as shown in Listing 23.9.

LISTING 23.9 **Disabling Outer Joins in Queries**

```
Set-SPAccessServiceApplication -Identity "Access Services"
-OuterJoinsAllowed:$false
```

You can use `-OuterJoinsAllowed` by itself to enable this setting or with a `$true` value, as shown in Listing 23.10.

LISTING 23.10 **Enabling Outer Joins in Queries**

```
Set-SPAccessServiceApplication -Identity "Access Services"
-OuterJoinsAllowed:$true
```

Allow or Restrict Nonremotable Queries

Scenario/Problem: You need to allow or restrict the use of non-remotable queries.

Solution: Use the `NonRemotableQueriesAllowed` switch parameter with the `Set-SPAccessServiceApplication` cmdlet.

Nonremotable queries are queries that cannot be remotely executed within the database. By default, the Access Services service application is configured to allow nonremotable queries. Because `NonRemotableQueriesAllowed` is a switch parameter, you can use it with a `$false` setting to disable nonremotable queries, as shown in Listing 23.11.

LISTING 23.11 **Disabling Nonremotable Queries**

```
Set-SPAccessServiceApplication -Identity "Access Services"
-NonRemotableQueriesAllowed:$false
```

You can use `-NonRemotableQueriesAllowed` by itself to enable this setting or with a `$true` value, as shown in Listing 23.12.

LISTING 23.12 **Enabling Nonremotable Queries**

```
Set-SPAccessServiceApplication -Identity "Access Services"
-NonRemotableQueriesAllowed:$true
```

NOTE When you are reviewing this setting in the Access Services service application settings within Central Administration, the check box label states "Remotable Queries Allowed." However, if this box is checked, it means that nonremotable queries are indeed allowed.

Throttle Access Services Memory Utilization

Scenario/Problem: You want to modify the amount of memory that Access Services can utilize.

Solution: Use the `PrivateBytesMax` parameter with the `Set-SPAccessServiceApplication` cmdlet.

By default, Access Services is configured to use up to 50% of the physical memory of the application server that is hosting the service application. This is denoted by a -1 value for the Maximum Private Bytes setting. To change this value, you can use the `PrivateBytesMax` parameter with a value between 1 and the maximum amount of physical memory available. Listing 23.13 shows a sample modification of memory usage using the `Set-SPAccessServiceApplication` cmdlet.

LISTING 23.13 **Modifying the Memory Usage of Access Services**

```
Set-SPAccessServiceApplication -Identity "Access Services"
-PrivateBytesMax 1024
```

If Access Services is heavily used within your SharePoint environment, you might want to allocate more memory to the service application. If the server that hosts Access Services also hosts other service applications, consider adding more memory to that server or splitting services onto dedicated servers. This depends on your overall utilization and SharePoint topology.

Throttle Session Memory Utilization

Scenario/Problem: You want to modify the amount of memory that Access Services can utilize per session.

Solution: Use the `SessionMemoryMax` parameter with the `Set-SPAccessServiceApplication` cmdlet.

By default, Access Services is configured to use up 64MB of memory per session. To change this value, you can use the `SessionMemoryMax` parameter with a value between 1 and 4095. Listing 23.14 shows a sample modification of session memory usage using the `Set-SPAccessServiceApplication` cmdlet.

LISTING 23.14 **Modifying the Session Memory Usage of Access Services**

```
Set-SPAccessServiceApplication -Identity "Access Services"
-SessionMemoryMax 50
```

This is the maximum amount of memory that a session will use. Normally, only a small amount is needed, so the default limit of 64MB should be plenty. If sessions are using more memory than expected, you might want to investigate what operations are being performed during typical sessions.

Configure User Sessions

Scenario/Problem: You want to modify the amount of sessions per user within Access Services.

Solution: Use the `SessionsPerUserMax` or `SessionsPerAnonymousUserMax` parameters with the `Set-SPAccessServiceApplication` cmdlet.

The `SessionsPerUserMax` and `SessionsPerAnonymousUserMax` settings determine the maximum number of sessions that can be created per user. When the limit is reached, older sessions are deleted to make room for new ones. The default per user is 10, whereas the default per anonymous user is 25. An entry of –1 denotes unlimited, and the valid range otherwise is 1 to the maximum integer value allowed. Listing 23.15 shows an example of setting both user session values.

LISTING 23.15 **Modifying the Number of Sessions Per User**

```
Set-SPAccessServiceApplication -Identity "Access Services"
-SessionsPerUserMax 5 -SessionsPerAnonymousUserMax 5
```

Stale sessions will indeed continue to take up resources until the cache timeout is reached. If users are constantly instantiating new sessions, you might want to decrease these maximum session settings.

Limit Template Sizes

Scenario/Problem: You want to modify the size limit the Access templates uploaded to SharePoint.

Solution: Use the `TemplateSizeMax` parameter with the `Set-SPAccessServiceApplication` cmdlet.

The `TemplateSizeMax` parameter can be used to configure the maximum size of an Access template. The default is 30MB. An entry of –1 denotes no limit, and a valid entry is any positive integer. Listing 23.16 shows an example of modifying the template size limit.

LISTING 23.16 **Modifying the Template Size Limit**

```
Set-SPAccessServiceApplication -Identity "Access Services"
-TemplateSizeMax 20
```

Similar to web applications limiting documents over 50MB, the Template Size setting, by default, limits the uploading of Access templates that are more than 30MB. Typically, Access templates should not become that large because usually no data is included.

This setting deals with only the uploading of Access templates that are .accdt files. This has nothing to do with Access Web Database files (.accdb) that can be published to Access Services from Access 2013.

Modify Access Services Databases

Scenario/Problem: You need to modify the databases and/or database servers used by Access Services.

Solution: Use the cmdlets listed in this section to change database servers, server groups, or databases themselves.

This chapter covers the basic or more common cmdlets for creating and using Access Services objects. For more advanced scripting and modifications of these objects, the following cmdlets are available:

- ▶ Get-SPAccessServicesDatabase
- ▶ Get-SPAccessServicesDatabaseServer
- ▶ Set-SPAccessServicesDatabaseServer
- ▶ Get-SPAccessServicesDatabaseServerGroup
- ▶ Get-SPAccessServicesDatabaseServerGroupMapping
- ▶ Set-SPAccessServicesDatabaseServerGroupMapping
- ▶ New-SPAccessServicesDatabaseServer
- ▶ Remove-SPAccessServicesDatabaseServer
- ▶ Reset-SPAccessServicesDatabasePassword

CHAPTER 24

Visio Graphics Services

This chapter explores the administrative aspects of Visio Graphics Services through the use of SharePoint PowerShell cmdlets.

Configure the Unattended Service Account

Scenario/Problem: You need to configure the unattended service account for Visio Graphics Services.

Solution: Use the `Set-SPVisioExternalData` cmdlet.

Visio Graphics Services uses the Secure Store Service to facilitate the use of an unattended service account. You must first create a Secure Store Service entry with an Application ID for Visio Graphics Services.

When an Application ID has been established, you can use the `Set-SPVisioExternalData` cmdlet to configure the unattended service account for Visio Graphic Services, as shown in Listing 24.1.

LISTING 24.1 **Configure the Unattended Service Account**

```
Set-SPVisioExternalData -VisioServiceApplication "Visio Graphics
Service" -UnattendedServiceAccountApplicationID "SSS Visio Graphics"
```

TIP Use the `Get-SPVisioExternalData` cmdlet to verify the unattended service account application ID entry.

Create a New Safe Data Provider

Scenario/Problem: You need to create a new safe data provider for Visio Graphics Services.

Solution: Use the `New-SPVisioSafeDataProvider` cmdlet.

The `New-SPVisioSafeDataProvider` cmdlet can be used to create a new safe data provider that Excel workbooks can access via a data connection. Provide the provider information and the Visio Graphics Service instance, as shown in Listing 24.2.

LISTING 24.2 **Create a New Safe Data Provider**

```
New-SPVisioSafeDataProvider -VisioServiceApplication "Visio Graphics
Service" -DataProviderID "Custom DB" -DataProviderType 6
```

-DataProviderID is an identifier for the data provider. -DataProviderType can be any of the following integer values:

> 1 - OLE DB
>
> 2 - SQL Server
>
> 3 - ODBC
>
> 4 - ODBC with DSN
>
> 5 - SharePoint List
>
> 6 - Custom

> **TIP** Verify third-party data provider documentation for the proper Data Provider ID and Data Provider Type to use.

Upon successful creation of the new safe data provider, a summary of the properties displays, as shown in Figure 24.1.

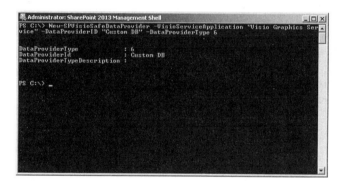

FIGURE 24.1 Creating a new safe data provider entry.

Notice that the DataProviderTypeDescription is blank. The New-SPVisioSafeData Provider cmdlet does not have a parameter to include a description. To update the description, you need to use the Set-SPVisioSafeDataProvider cmdlet.

Display All Safe Data Providers

> **Scenario/Problem:** You need to display all safe data providers configured for a Visio Graphics Service.

Solution: Use the Get-SPVisioSafeDataProvider cmdlet with the VisioServiceApplication parameter.

Using the `Get-SPVisioSafeDataProvider` cmdlet with the VisioServiceApplication parameter, as shown in Listing 24.3, displays all configured safe data providers.

LISTING 24.3 **Display All Safe Data Providers**

```
Get-SPVisioSafeDataProvider -VisioServiceApplication "Visio Graphics
Service"
```

Get a Specific Safe Data Provider

Scenario/Problem: You need to obtain a specific safe data provider reference.

Solution: Use the `Get-SPVisioSafeDataProvider` cmdlet.

The `Get-SPVisioSafeDataProvider` cmdlet can be used to retrieve a specific safe data provider using the `VisioServiceApplication` and data provider parameters, as shown in Listing 24.4.

LISTING 24.4 **Assigning a Variable to a Specific Data Provider**

```
$dataProvider =
Get-SPVisioSafeDataProvider -VisioServiceApplication "Visio Graphics
Service" -DataProviderID "Custom DB" -DataProviderType 6
```

This cmdlet uses both the `DataProviderID` and the `DataProviderType` to identify the safe data provider. If one is excluded, no results are returned.

Remove a Safe Data Provider

Scenario/Problem: You need to remove a safe data provider from Visio Graphics Services.

Solution: Use the `Remove-SPVisioSafeDataProvider` cmdlet.

The `Remove-SPVisioSafeDataProvider` cmdlet enables you to remove a specific safe data provider from Visio Graphics Services. This cmdlet uses both the `DataProviderID` and the `DataProviderType` to identify the safe data provider, as shown in Listing 24.5.

LISTING 24.5 **Example Script for Removing a Safe Data Provider**

```
Remove-SPVisioSafeDataProvider -VisioServiceApplication "Visio
Graphics Service" -DataProviderID "Custom DB" -DataProviderType 6
```

Setting the Description of a Data Provider

Scenario/Problem: You need to enter a description for a safe provider entry.

Solution: Use the `Set-SPVisioSafeDataProvider` cmdlet.

The only purpose of the `Set-SPVisioSafeDataProvider` cmdlet is to add or change the description of a specific safe data provider for a Visio Graphics Service Application. This cmdlet uses both the `DataProviderID` and the `DataProviderType` to identify the safe data provider, as shown in Listing 24.6.

LISTING 24.6 **Setting the Description of a Safe Data Provider**

```
Set-SPVisioSafeDataProvider -VisioServiceApplication "Visio Graphics
Service" -DataProviderID "Custom DB" -DataProviderType 6 -Description
"Custom DB Provider"
```

TIP Use the `Get-SPVisioSafeDataProvider` to verify the description entry or modification.

Configuring Visio Performance Settings

Scenario/Problem: You need to modify performance properties of Visio Graphics Services.

Solution: Use the `Set-SPVisioPerformance` cmdlet to configure the performance settings.

One of the unique characteristics of the `Set-SPVisioPerformance` cmdlet is that it requires all the parameters for configuring the Visio Graphics Service. Therefore, you must provide a value for each setting, as shown in Listing 24.7.

LISTING 24.7 **Configuring the Visio Performance Settings**

```
Set-SPVisioPerformance -VisioServiceApplication "Visio Graphics
Service" -MaxDiagramCacheAge 30 -MaxDiagramSize 5 -MaxRecalcDuration
60 -MinDiagramCacheAge 10
```

The -MaxDiagramCacheAge parameter determines the maximum number of minutes a diagram should be cached. A longer cache age reduces memory and CPU utilization because the diagrams are not refreshed as often. The default value is 60 minutes, but the valid range of values for this parameter is 0 to 34,560 minutes (equating to 24 days).

The -MaxDiagramSize parameter determines the largest number of megabytes a Visio diagram can be to still be processed by the Visio Graphics Service. The default value is 5MB, but the valid range of values for this parameter is 1 to 50MB.

The -MaxRecalcDuration parameter determines the maximum number of seconds that the Visio Graphics Service should spend recalculating a diagram. The default is 60 seconds; the parameter range is 1 to 120 seconds. Any recalculations that take longer than this setting time out.

The -MinDiagramCacheAge parameter determines the minimum number of minutes a diagram should be cached. A longer cache age reduces memory and CPU utilization because the diagrams are not refreshed as often. The default value is 5 minutes, but the valid range of values for this parameter is 0 to 34,560 minutes (equating to 24 days).

> **TIP** To force a fixed cache duration, set the MaxDiagramCacheAge and MinDiagramCacheAge to the same values.

CHAPTER 25

Word Automation Services

This chapter explores the administrative aspects of Word Services through the use of SharePoint PowerShell cmdlets. Technically, the service application is Word Automation Services, but to be consistent with the other Office applications, this book calls it Word Services.

Similar to Access Services, Word Services is pretty light in regard to its associated PowerShell commands. Essentially, only one cmdlet is used often to configure Word Services settings. However, because many options can be configured separately, this chapter describes the scenarios for those settings.

Configure the Conversion Processes

Scenario/Problem: You need to modify the number of conversion processes on each server running Word Services.

Solution: Use the `ActiveProcesses` parameter with the `Set-SPWordConversionServiceApplication` cmdlet.

The `ActiveProcesses` parameter determines the how many active conversion processes can occur on each server running the Word Services service application. The default value is 8 processes. The valid entries range from 1 to 1000. Listing 25.1 shows a sample modification of the active conversion processes.

LISTING 25.1 **Setting the Active Conversion Processes**

```
Set-SPWordConversionServiceApplication
-Identity "Word Automation Services" -ActiveProcesses 5
```

TIP The default identity of the Word Service application is "Word Automation Services." To find the correct name or GUID, use `Get-SPServiceApplication`.

Configure Conversion Throughput

Scenario/Problem: You need to configure the throughput for the Word Services conversions.

Solution: Use the `TimerJobFrequency` and `ConversionsPerInstance` parameters with the `Set-SPWordConversionServiceApplication` cmdlet.

The conversion throughput parameters `TimerJobFrequency` and `ConversionsPerInstance` correspond to the Word Services configuration settings, as shown in Figure 25.1.

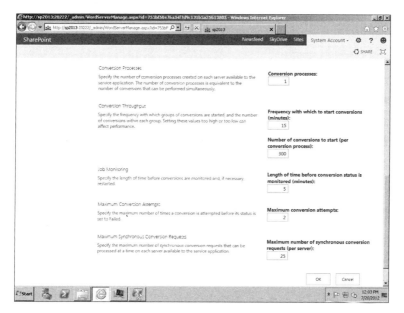

FIGURE 25.1 Conversion throughput configuration settings in Central Administration.

> **TIP** To get to these properties, from Central Admin, click on the Manage Service Applications link under Application Management. Locate the Word Services entry and highlight the connection (the indented instance) and then click on the Properties button from the top ribbon bar.

The `TimerJobFrequency` parameter determines how often the conversion process should be started using the corresponding service timer job. The default is 15 minutes, and the valid range can be any number of minutes between 1 and 59.

The `ConversionsPerInstance` parameter determines how many conversions can be processed per instance. The number of instances can be configured using the `ActiveProcesses` parameter, as explained in the previous section. The default value is 12 conversions.

Listing 25.2 shows a sample command line for setting the conversion throughput values.

LISTING 25.2 **Setting the Conversion Throughput Values**

```
Set-SPWordConversionServiceApplication
-Identity "Word Automation Services"
-TimerJobFrequency 5 -ConversionsPerInstance 100
```

The values for throughput should be modified based on usage of Word Services within your organization. Heavy usage might warrant more frequent timer job execution. Increasing the number of minutes for the timer might may warrant an increase in conversions per instance; however, increasing these values could cause performance issues. Use these values along with the active processes to balance the usage and optimize throughput.

Configure Supported Document Formats for Conversion

Scenario/Problem: You need to modify the supported document formats for Word Services.

Solution: Use the `AddSupportedFormats` and `RemoveSupportedFormats` parameters with the `Set-SPWordConversionServiceApplication` cmdlet.

By default, all available document file formats are supported within Word Services. You can use the `AddSupportedFormats` or `RemoveSupportedFormats` parameters with the `Set-SPWordConversionServiceApplication` cmdlet to modify which set of formats is supported.

Both of these parameters take a comma-separated list of valid document formats. The recognized values are as follows:

- ▶ `docx`: Open XML document. This essentially is any Word 2010 or Word 2007 document and includes `.docx`, `.docm`, `.dotx`, and `.dotm` documents.
- ▶ `doc`: Word 97–2003 documents. Provides support for older Word documents with `.doc` and `.dot` extensions.
- ▶ `rtf`: Rich Text Format. Supports only `.rtf` files.
- ▶ `mht`: Web page. Any HTML-based web page, including `.htm`, `.html`, `.mht`, and `.mhtml` documents.
- ▶ `xml`: Word 2003 XML document. Any Word 2003 document saved as an `.xml` file.

As an example of how these parameters operate, removing `doc` also removes support it for `.dot` documents. The supported formats are grouped together and cannot be broken apart. These groups correspond to the available options available through Central Administration, as shown in Figure 25.2. Listing 25.3 shows sample command lines.

LISTING 25.3 **Modifying the Supported File Formats**

```
Set-SPWordConversionServiceApplication
-Identity "Word Automation Services" -RemoveSupportedFormats rtf,mht
Set-SPWordConversionServiceApplication
-Identity "Word Automation Services" -AddSupportedFormats docx,doc
```

FIGURE 25.2 Supported document options for Word Services.

You can use quotation marks around a single file format; however, when you are providing a comma-separated list of formats, you cannot use quotation marks. No errors are presented, although the operation cannot modify the settings.

> **TIP** When scripting out supported file format operations, use the `ClearSupportedFormats` parameter first to start with a clean slate; then just add the supported types. This ensures that any unsupported types do not remain active.

Modify Database Information

Scenario/Problem: You need to modify the database that Word Services should use.

Solution: Use the database parameters with the `Set-SPWordConversionServiceApplication` cmdlet.

Three database parameters can be used to configure the database settings for Word Services: `DatabaseServer`, `DatabaseName`, and `DatabaseCredential`. The `DatabaseCredential` parameter is used only if the authorization is performed through SQL authentication. Even though all these parameters are optional overall, if the

DatabaseCredential parameter is used, then DatabaseServer and DatabaseName become required. Listing 25.4 shows a sample modification of the database settings.

LISTING 25.4 **Changing the Database Configuration for Word Services**

```
Set-SPWordConversionServiceApplication
-Identity "Word Automation Services" -DatabaseServer SP2010
-DatabaseName WordServices -DatabaseCredential (Get-Credential)
```

TIP Use inline credentials instead of (Get-Credential). See Chapter 2, "PowerShell Basics," for more details.

If the database described within the DatabaseName parameter does not exist, it is created automatically.

TIP Use the database parameters to create a new database without the GUID. Delete the old WordAutomationServices_GUID database afterward.

Modify Job Monitoring

Scenario/Problem: You need to modify the job monitoring timeout value.

Solution: Use the ConversionTimeout parameters with the Set-SPWordConversionServiceApplication cmdlet.

The job-monitoring configuration setting is modified using the ConversionTimeOut parameter. This value is the number of minutes a conversion should be in progress before the timer job restarts the conversion. The default is 5 minutes. The valid range of values is 1 to 60 minutes. Listing 25.5 shows a sample modification of the job monitoring setting.

LISTING 25.5 **Changing the Job Monitoring Timeout Setting**

```
Set-SPWordConversionServiceApplication
-Identity "Word Automation Services"
-ConversionTimeout 10
```

This is different from the actual configurations that determine how long a conversion can be nonresponsive or how long a conversion should run. You can modify those values using the parameters explained in the next section.

Modify Conversion Timeouts

Scenario/Problem: You need to modify conversion timeout values either for running or nonresponsive conversions.

Solution: Use the `KeepAliveTimeout` or `MaximumConversionTime` parameters with the `Set-SPWordConversionServiceApplication` cmdlet.

To confuse matters, the `ConversionTimeout` parameter explained in the previous section deals with job monitoring, not the timeouts of conversion processing. Use the `KeepAliveTimeout` parameter to determine how many seconds a process can be nonresponsive before it is terminated. The valid values for this setting are 10 to 60 seconds, and the default is 30 seconds.

Use the `MaximumConversionTime` parameter to determine how long a conversion should continue running. The default is 300 seconds, whereas the range starts at 60 seconds and can go up to the maximum allowed integer value. Listing 25.6 shows a sample modification of the conversion timeout setting.

LISTING 25.6 **Changing the Conversion Timeout Settings**

```
Set-SPWordConversionServiceApplication -Identity "Word Automation
Services" -KeepAliveTimeout 45 -MaximumConversionTime 120
```

These values cannot be configured through the service application settings in Central Administration. As of this writing, they are available only via the `Set-SPWordConversionServiceApplication` cmdlet.

Modify the Maximum Conversion Attempts

Scenario/Problem: You need to modify the maximum conversion attempts in Word Services.

Solution: Use the `MaximumConversionAttempts` parameter with the `Set-SPWordConversionServiceApplication` cmdlet.

Use the `MaximumConversionAttempts` parameter to configure how many attempts should be taken before a conversion is considered a failure. The default is 2 (attempts), and the range of valid values is 1 to 10. Listing 25.7 shows a sample modification of the maximum conversion attempts setting.

LISTING 25.7 **Changing the Maximum Conversion Attempts Setting**

```
Set-SPWordConversionServiceApplication -Identity "Word Automation
Services" -MaximumConversionAttempts 3
```

The default is two attempts, but three seems like a normal setting. Anything more than five is probably too optimistic. If the conversion fails after three times, there is a 90% chance that it will continue to fail.

Modify the Maximum Memory Usage

Scenario/Problem: You need to modify the maximum memory usage of Word Services.

Solution: Use the `MaximumMemoryUsage` parameter with the `Set-SPWordConversionServiceApplication` cmdlet.

Use the `MaximumMemoryUsage` parameter to configure how much memory Word Services can use on the server. The default is `100` (percent), whereas the range of valid values is `10` to `100`. Listing 25.8 shows a sample modification of the maximum memory usage setting.

LISTING 25.8 **Changing the Maximum Memory Usage to 50%**

```
Set-SPWordConversionServiceApplication
-Identity "Word Automation Services" -MaximumMemoryUsage 50
```

Most service applications like to use as much memory as possible (as defined by their default memory settings). Although most settings determine the maximum amount that can be used, you should monitor usage and available memory on your application servers to determine how to balance these settings across service applications.

Disable Word 97–2003 Document Scanning

Scenario/Problem: You want to disable extra checks on Word 97–2003 documents loaded by Word Services.

Solution: Use the `DisableBinaryFileScan` parameter with the `Set-SPWordConversionServiceApplication` cmdlet.

`DisableBinaryFileScan` is a switch parameter. By default, it is `false`, and Word Services performs additional checks on legacy Word documents (Word

97–2003). If you trust all sources of Word documents, you can disable this additional scanning by using Set-SPWordConversionServiceApplication with the DisableBinaryFileScan switch parameter, as shown in Listing 25.9.

LISTING 25.9 **Disabling the Scanning of Word 97–2003 Documents**

```
Set-SPWordConversionServiceApplication
-Identity "Word Automation Services" -DisableBinaryFileScan
```

As long as all sources are trusted, it is a good idea to disable scanning to improve performance of Word Services against those documents. To enable scanning, use the same parameter with a $false value, as shown in Listing 25.10.

LISTING 25.10 **Enabling the Scanning of Word 97–2003 Documents**

```
Set-SPWordConversionServiceApplication
-Identity "Word Automation Services" -DisableBinaryFileScan:$false
```

Disable Embedded Fonts in Conversions

Scenario/Problem: You want to disable the use of embedded fonts within Word document conversions.

Solution: Use the DisableEmbeddedFonts parameter with the Set-SPWordConversionServiceApplication cmdlet.

DisableEmbeddedFonts is a switch parameter. By default, it is false, and Word Services supports the conversion of embedded fonts within Word documents. You can disable this support by using Set-SPWordConversionServiceApplication with the DisableEmbeddedFonts switch parameter, as shown in Listing 25.11.

LISTING 25.11 **Disabling Embedded Font Support**

```
Set-SPWordConversionServiceApplication
-Identity "Word Automation Services" -DisableEmbeddedFonts
```

Unless you are experiencing issues with embedded fonts, you should be able to keep this setting enabled. To enable embedded font support, use the same parameter with a $false value, as shown in Listing 25.12.

LISTING 25.12 **Enabling Embedded Font Support**

```
Set-SPWordConversionServiceApplication
-Identity "Word Automation Services" -DisableEmbeddedFonts:$false
```

Modify the Recycle Threshold

Scenario/Problem: You need to modify the recycle threshold of the conversion processes in Word Services.

Solution: Use the `RecycleProcessThreshold` parameter with the `Set-SPWordConversionServiceApplication` cmdlet.

The `RecycleProcessThreshold` parameter enables you to specify the number of documents each conversion process can convert before the process is recycled. The default value is 100 (documents), whereas the valid range of values is 1 to 1000. Listing 25.13 shows a sample threshold modification.

LISTING 25.13 **Changing the Recycle Threshold**

```
Set-SPWordConversionServiceApplication
-Identity "Word Automation Services" -RecycleProcessThreshold 200
```

CHAPTER 26

Office Web Apps

This chapter explores new cmdlets in SharePoint 2013 that can be used to configure Web Application Open Platform Interface Protocol (WOPI) applications in SharePoint. The SharePoint 2013 WOPI cmdlets enable you to create new bindings and configure WOPI settings.

From the WOPI specification by Microsoft, "WOPI defines a set of operations that enables a client to access and change files stored by a server. This allows the client to render files and provide file editing functionality for files stored by the server."

The full specification and details can be found here: http://msdn.microsoft.com/en-us/library/hh622722(v=office.12).aspx.

Essentially, the WOPI provides a method of rendering specific types of files in a browser without the need for a client application. In other words, you can render Word documents within Internet Explorer without having Microsoft Word installed on your machine.

Although the WOPI settings are generic and are used for any WOPI-type application, server, and/or services, the Microsoft Office WOPI applications are named Office Web Apps. To use Office Web Apps locally with SharePoint 2013, you must have a dedicated server running Office Web Apps Server.

Create a New WOPI Binding in SharePoint

Scenario/Problem: You need to create a new binding to associate a file name extension with an application within your SharePoint farm.

Solution: Use the `New-SPWOPIBinding` cmdlet.

The `New-SPWOPIBinding` cmdlet creates a new binding to associate file types or applications with SharePoint. Essentially, if you have an Office Web App server running, you simply need to execute this cmdlet with the server name, as shown in Listing 26.1.

LISTING 26.1 **Creating the WOPI Binding in SharePoint**

```
New-SPWOPIBinding -ServerName "Office.mycompany.com"
```

This automatically associates the supported file extensions and applications within SharePoint. The current supported applications are Word, Excel, PowerPoint, and OneNote.

You can also use the `-Application` parameter to bind a specific application, as shown in Listing 26.2. The valid parameter values are as follows:

- ▶ Excel
- ▶ OneNote
- ▶ PowerPoint
- ▶ Word

LISTING 26.2 **Creating the WOPI Binding for a Specific Application**

```
New-SPWOPIBinding -ServerName "Office.mycompany.com" - Application "Word"
```

Review Current SharePoint WOPI Bindings

Scenario/Problem: You would like to see the WOPI bindings generated on your SharePoint farm.

Solution: Use the `Get-SPWOPIBinding` cmdlet.

You can use the `Get-SPWOPIBinding` cmdlet to retrieve a list of bindings that were created as a result of the `New-SPWOPIBinding` cmdlet, explained in the previous section. You can use the cmdlet without any parameters, or you can provide one or more of the following parameters to narrow the list:

▶ `Action`: String that specifies a specific action to return (such as `view` or `edit`)

▶ `Application`: String that specifies a specific application to return (such as `Excel`)

▶ `Extension`: String that specifies a specific file extension to return (such as `doc` or `xls`)

▶ `Server`: String that specifies a specific WOPI server to return

▶ `WOPIZone`: String that specifies a specific zone to return

TIP Use the `Get-SPWOPIBinding` with specific parameters in conjunction with the `Set-SPWOPIBinding` cmdlet to implement default actions as explained in the next section.

Configure the Default Action for an Application

Scenario/Problem: You need to configure the default action for an application.

Solution: Use the `Set-SPWOPIBinding` cmdlet.

The `Set-SPWOPIBinding` cmdlet is used to set the default action of applications. This is achieved by providing the `-DefaultAction` switch parameter, along with a `WOPIBinding` object via the `-Identity` parameter.

Use the `Get-SPWOPIBinding` cmdlet, explained in the previous section, to set a variable to a specific binding or pipe the results into the `Set-SPWOPIBinding` cmdlet, as shown in Listing 26.3.

LISTING 26.3 **Configuring the Default Action for Excel Documents in SharePoint**

```
Get-SPWOPIBinding -Action "View" -Application "Excel"
| Set-SPWOPIBinding -DefaultAction:$true
```

Remove WOPI Bindings from SharePoint

Scenario/Problem: You need to remove WOPI bindings from SharePoint.

Solution: Use the `Remove-SPWOPIBinding` cmdlet.

The `Remove-SPWOPIBinding` cmdlet has three different parameter sets that can be used to remove bindings. The simplest set removes all bindings and needs only the `-All` switch parameter, as shown in Listing 26.4.

LISTING 26.4 **Removing All WOPI Bindings from SharePoint**

```
Remove-SPWOPIBinding -All
```

Provide a specific binding using the identity pipe parameter to remove a specific binding (as shown in Listing 26.5) or simply provide the same parameters to `Remove-SPWOPIBinding` as you would to get the binding (as shown in Listing 26.6).

LISTING 26.5 **Removing a Specific Binding Using the Identity Pipe**

```
Get-SPWOPIBinding -Application "Excel" | Remove-SPWOPIBinding
```

LISTING 26.6 **Removing a Specific Binding Using Parameters**

```
Remove-SPWOPIBinding -Application "Excel"
```

Use the following parameters to identify a specific binding:

- ▶ `Action`: String that specifies a specific action to return (such as `view` or `edit`)
- ▶ `Application`: String that specifies a specific application to return (such as `Excel`)
- ▶ `Extension`: String that specifies a specific file extension to return (such as `doc` or `xls`)
- ▶ `Server`: String that specifies a specific WOPI server to return
- ▶ `WOPIZone`: String that specifies a specific zone to return

Configure the WOPI SharePoint Zone

Scenario/Problem: You need to configure the zone that SharePoint will use to navigate the browser to the WOPI application.

Solution: Use the `Set-SPWOPIZone` cmdlet.

The `Set-SPWOPIZone` cmdlet is used solely to configure the zone in which SharePoint uses to navigate the browser to the WOPI application. The zone is specified using the `-Zone` parameter and can be one of the following values:

▶ `Internal-HTTP`

▶ `Internal-HTTPS`

▶ `External-HTTP`

▶ `External-HTTPS`

Disable Certain WOPI Actions

Scenario/Problem: You need to disable certain WOPI actions within SharePoint such that other Office document functionality functions properly (e.g. Excel Services to view workbooks instead of launching WOPI).

Solution: Use the `New-SPWOPISuppressionSetting` cmdlet.

The `New-SPWOPISuppressionSetting` cmdlet is used to disable Office Web App functionality for the specified action, file extension, and/or programmatic identifier. You can view the current bindings using the `Get-SPWOPIBinding` cmdlet and retrieve the available values for the parameters. Typically, the `-Action` and `-Extension` parameters are used together to suppress an action for a particular document type, as shown in Listing 26.7.

LISTING 26.7 **Suppressing an Action on a Specific File Extension**

```
New-SPWOPISuppressionSetting -Action "View" -Extension "xls"
```

To view current suppression settings, use the `Get-SPWOPISuppressionSetting` cmdlet without any parameters. You can also remove any suppression setting by using the `Remove-SPWOPISuppressionSetting` cmdlet with the action and extension or by providing the identity of the specific suppression setting.

Resolve Invalid Proof Signature

Scenario/Problem: You discover that WOPI functionality is not functioning and find "Invalid Proof Signature" messages within the SharePoint logs.

Solution: Use the `Update-SPWOPIProofKey` cmdlet with the WOPI server name.

WOPI uses a public key to for communication between the SharePoint farm and the Office Web Apps server. Sometimes keys become unsynchronized and need to be reset. Use the `Update-SPWOPIProofKey` cmdlet with the optional `-ServerName` parameter to update the public key and resolve any invalid proof signature issues. Listing 26.8 shows an example.

LISTING 26.8 **Updating the WOPI Public Key**

```
Update-SPWOPIProofKey -ServerName "Office.mycompany.com"
```

APPENDIX A

stsadm Versus SharePoint PowerShell

This appendix presents a guide to the previous stsadm operations and the new SharePoint PowerShell cmdlet replacements. Because stsadm is being phased out, the new PowerShell cmdlets will become the standard administration method.

A Operations

stsadm Operation	SharePoint 2013 Management Shell Cmdlet
Activatefeature	Enable-SPFeature
Activateformtemplate	Enable-SPInfoPathFormTemplate
Addalternatedomain	New-SPAlternateUrl
Addcontentdb	Mount-SPContentDatabaseNew-SPContentDatabase
Adddataconnectionfile	Install-SPDataConnectionFile
Add-ecsfiletrustedlocation	New-SPExcelFileLocation
Add-ecssafedataprovider	New-SPExcelDataProvider
Add-ecstrusteddata connectionlibrary	New-SPExcelDataConnection Library
Add-ecsuserdefinedfunction	New-SPExcelUserDefinedFunction
Addexemptuseragent	Add-SPInfoPathUserAgent
Addpath	New-SPManagedPath
Addsolution	Add-SPSolution
Addtemplate	Install-SPWebTemplate
Adduser	New-SPUser
Addwppack	Install-SPWebPartPack
Addzoneurl	New-SPAlternateUrl
Allowuserformwebserviceproxy	Set-SPInfoPathWebServiceProxy
Allowwebserviceproxy	Set-SPInfoPathWebServiceProxy
Authentication	Set-SPWebApplication

B Operations

stsadm Operation	SharePoint 2013 Management Shell Cmdlet
Backup	Backup-SPConfigurationDatabaseBackup-SPFarmBackup-SPSite
Backuphistory	Get-SPBackupHistory

C Operations

stsadm Operation	SharePoint 2013 Management Shell Cmdlet
Createadminvs	New-SPCentralAdministration
Createsite	New-SPSite
Createsiteinnewdb	New-SPSite
Createweb	New-SPWeb

D Operations

stsadm Operation	SharePoint 2013 Management Shell Cmdlet
Deactivatefeature	Disable-SPFeature
Deactivateformtemplate	Disable-SPInfoPathFormTemplate
Deletealternatedomain	Remove-SPAlternateUrl
Deleteconfigdb	Remove-SPConfigurationDatabase
Deletecontentdb	Dismount-SPContentDatabase
Deletepath	Remove-SPManagedPath
Deletesite	Remove-SPSite
Deletesolution	Remove-SPSolution
Deletetemplate	Uninstall-SPWebTemplate
Deleteuser	Remove-SPUser
Deleteweb	Remove-SPWeb
Deletewppack	Uninstall-SPWebPartPack
Deletezoneurl	Remove-SPAlternateUrl
Deploysolution	Install-SPSolution
Deploywppack	Install-SPWebPartPack
Displaysolution	Get-SPSolution

E Operations

stsadm Operation	SharePoint 2013 Management Shell Cmdlet
Editcontentdeploymentpath	Set-SPContentDeploymentPath
Enumalternatedomains	Get-SPAlternateURL
Enumcontentdbs	Get-SPContentDatabase
Enumdataconnectionfiledependants	Get-SPDataConnectionFileDependent
Enumdataconnectionfiles	Get-SPDataConnectionFile
Enumexemptuseragents	Get-SPInfoPathUserAgent
Enumformtemplates	Get-SPInfoPathFormTemplate
Enumservices	Get-SPServiceInstance
Enumsites	Get-SPSite
Enumsolutions	Get-SPSolution
Enumsubwebs	Get-SPWeb
Enumtemplates	Get-SPWebTemplate
Enumusers	Get-SPUser
Enumwppacks	Get-SPWebPartPack
Enumzoneurls	Get-SPAlternateURL
Execadmsvcjobs	Start-SPAdminJob
Export	Export-SPWeb
Extendvs	New-SPWebApplication
Extendvsinwebfarm	New-SPWebApplicationExtension

G Operations

stsadm Operation	SharePoint 2013 Management Shell Cmdlet
Getadminport	Get-SPWebApplication
Getdataconnectionfileproperty	Get-SPDataConnectionFile
Getformtemplateproperty	Get-SPInfoPathFormTemplate
Getproperty	Get-SPFarmConfigGet-SPTimerJob Disable-SPTimerJobEnable-SPTimerJob Set-SPTimerJobStart-SPTimerJob
Getsitelock	Get-SPSiteAdministration
Geturlzone	Get-SPAlternateURL

I Operations

stsadm Operation	SharePoint 2013 Management Shell Cmdlet
Import	Import-SPWeb
Installfeature	Install-SPFeature

L Operations

stsadm Operation	SharePoint 2013 Management Shell cmdlet
Listlogginglevels	Get-SPLogLevel
Listregisteredsecuritytrimmers	Get-SPEnterpriseSearchSecurityTrimmer

M Operations

stsadm Operation	SharePoint 2013 Management Shell Cmdlet
Mergecontentdbs	Move-SPSite
Migrateuser	Move-SPUser

O, P, and Q Operations

stsadm Operation	SharePoint 2013 Management Shell Cmdlet
Osearch	SPEnterpriseSearchServiceSPEnterpriseSearch ServiceInstance
Osearchdiacriticsensitive	SPEnterpriseSearchServiceApplication
Provisionservice	Start-SPServiceInstance
Quiesceformtemplate	Stop-SPInfoPathFormTemplate

R Operations

stsadm Operation	SharePoint 2013 Management Shell Cmdlet
Reconvertallformtemplates	Update-SPInfoPathFormTemplate
Registersecuritytrimmer	New-SPEnterpriseSearchSecurityTrimmer
Removedataconnectionfile	Uninstall-SPDataConnectionFile
Remove-ecsfiletrustedlocation	Remove-SPExcelFileLocation
Remove-ecssafedataprovider	Remove-SPExcelDataProvider

stsadm Operation	SharePoint 2013 Management Shell Cmdlet
Remove-ecstrusteddataconnection library	Remove-SPExcelDataConnectionLibrary
Remove-ecsuserdefinedfunction	Remove-SPExcelFileLocation
Removeexemptuseragent	Remove-SPInfoPathUserAgent
Removeformtemplate	Uninstall-SPInfoPathFormTemplate
Renameserver	Rename-SPServer
Renamesite	Set-SPSite
Renameweb	Set-SPWeb
Restore	Restore-SPFarmRestore-SPSite
Retractsolution	Uninstall-SPSolution
Runcontentdeploymentjob	Start-SPContentDeploymentJob

S Operations

stsadm Operation	SharePoint 2013 Management Shell Cmdlet
Scanforfeatures	Install-SPFeature
Setadminport	Set-SPCentralAdministration
Setconfigdb	Connect-SPConfigurationDatabase
Setcontentdeploymentjobschedule	Set-SPContentDeploymentJob
Setdataconnectionfileproperty	Set-SPDataConnectionFile
Set-ecsexternaldata	Set-SPExcelFileLocation
Set-ecsloadbalancing	Set-SPExcelServiceApplication
Set-ecsmemoryutilization	Set-SPExcelServiceApplication
Set-ecssecurity	Set-SPExcelServiceApplication
Set-ecssessionmanagement	Set-SPExcelServiceApplication
Set-ecsworkbookcache	Set-SPExcelServiceApplication
Setformtemplateproperty	Set-SPInfoPathFormTemplate
Setlogginglevel	Set-SPLogLevel
Setproperty	SPFarmConfig
	SPTimerJob
Setsitelock	Set-SPSiteAdministration
Setsiteuseraccountdirectorypath	Get-SPSiteSubscriptionNew-SPSiteSubscriptionRemove-SPSiteSubscription
Setworkflowconfig	Set-SPWorkflowConfig
Siteowner	Set-SPSiteAdministration
Syncsolution	Install-SPSolution

U Operations

stsadm Operation	SharePoint 2013 Management Shell Cmdlet
Unextendvs	Remove-SPWebApplication
Uninstallfeature	Uninstall-SPFeature
Unquiesceformtemplate	Start-SPInfoPathFormTemplate
Unregistersecuritytrimmer	Remove-SPEnterpriseSearchSecurityTrimmer
Updateaccountpassword	Set-SPManagedAccount
Upgradeformtemplate	Install-SPInfoPathFormTemplate
Upgradesolution	Update-SPSolution
Uploadformtemplate	Install-SPInfoPathFormTemplate
Userrole	SPUser

V Operations

stsadm Operation	SharePoint 2013 Management Shell Cmdlet
Verifyformtemplate	Test-SPInfoPathFormTemplate

APPENDIX B

Upgrade and Migration

This appendix presents several SharePoint useful cmdlets for the upgrade and migration process when migrating from MOSS 2007 or SharePoint 2010 to SharePoint 2013.

Test-SPContentDatabase

When performing a SharePoint migration, part of the operation is to back up the MOSS 2007 or SharePoint 2010 content database(s) and then restore them on your SharePoint 2013 SQL Server. You then test the content database(s) against your new SharePoint 2013 web application to identify any issues.

The syntax for this scenario follows:

```
Test-SPContentDatabase -Name <name of content database>
-WebApplication <name of web application to test against>
```

By default, the current SQL Server instance is used, but you can specify an instance by using the -ServerInstance parameter and passing in the SQL Server instance.

Upgrade-SPContentDatabase

After the content database has been tested and all issues have been resolved, it can be attached to the SharePoint farm using the Mount-SPContentDatabase cmdlet. The upgrade command will not execute until the content database is actually attached. At that point, you can execute the upgrade command using the following syntax:

```
Upgrade-SPContentDatabase -Name <name of content database>
-WebApplication <name of web application hosting content
database>
```

Again, by default, the current SQL Server instance is used, but you can specify an instance by using the -ServerInstance parameter and passing in the SQL Server instance.

Upgrade-SPFarm

To initiate the upgrade process on the local farm, use the `Upgrade-SPFarm` cmdlet. No parameters are required, so you can run this as is.

```
Upgrade-SPFarm
```

Test-SPSite

You must ensure that all site collections are considered healthy. You can run health analyzer tests against a site collection by using `Test-SPSite` and providing the URL of the site collection as the `Identity`.

```
Test-SPSite -Identity <URL or GUID of Site Collection> [-RuleId <rule
GUID>] [-RunAlways <optional switch parameter>]
```

Repair-SPSite

After testing a site collection, if repairs need to be made, you can use the `Repair-SPSite` cmdlet, which has similar parameters as the `Test-SPSite` cmdlet.

```
Repair-SPSite -Identity <URL or GUID of Site Collection> [-RuleId
<rule GUID>] [-RunAlways <optional switch parameter>]
```

Upgrade-SPSite

To start the upgrade process on a particular site collection, use the `Upgrade-SPSite` cmdlet and provide the GUID or URL for the `-Identity` parameter.

```
Upgrade-SPSite -Identity <URL or GUID of Site Collection>
[-Unthrottled] [-VersionUpgrade]
```

The `-Unthrottled` switch parameter acts as a "force" command and performs the upgrade on the specified site collection, regardless of how many site collections are being upgraded. The `-VersionUpgrade` switch parameter upgrades the site collection to the next build level (for example, from 12 to 14, or from 14 to 15).

Additional Upgrade Cmdlets

In addition to the common upgrade cmdlets for SharePoint migration, the following cmdlets are available for more granular upgrading:

- ▶ `Get-SPPendingUpgradeActions`
- ▶ `Get-SPSiteUpgradeSessionInfo`

- Get-SPUpgradeActions
- Remove-SPSiteUpgradeSessionInfo
- Request-SPUpgradeEvaluationSite
- Copy-SPSite

APPENDIX C

Enterprise Search Reference

This appendix presents all available Enterprise Search–related cmdlets. Enterprise Search consists of many areas, including crawling, querying, and metadata, and thus has a plethora of cmdlets.

Administrative

Only two cmdlets fall into this classification:

- ▶ Get-SPEnterpriseSearchStatus
- ▶ New-SPEnterpriseSearchAdminComponent

Crawling

The crawling cmdlets are used to tweak the crawl settings and configurations. The Get-based cmdlets are listed here:

- ▶ Get-SPEnterpriseSearchCrawlContentSource
- ▶ Get-SPEnterpriseSearchCrawlCustomConnector
- ▶ Get-SPEnterpriseSearchCrawlDatabase
- ▶ Get-SPEnterpriseSearchCrawlExtension
- ▶ Get-SPEnterpriseSearchCrawlMapping
- ▶ Get-SPEnterpriseSearchCrawlRule

Create new crawl objects (such as components, content sources, and databases) using these cmdlets:

- ▶ New-SPEnterpriseSearchCrawlComponent
- ▶ New-SPEnterpriseSearchCrawlContentSource
- ▶ New-SPEnterpriseSearchCrawlCustomConnector
- ▶ New-SPEnterpriseSearchCrawlDatabase

▶ New-SPEnterpriseSearchCrawlExtension

▶ New-SPEnterpriseSearchCrawlMapping

▶ New-SPEnterpriseSearchCrawlRule

You can remove crawl objects, permissions, and rules using these cmdlets:

▶ Remove-SPEnterpriseSearchCrawlContentSource

▶ Remove-SPEnterpriseSearchCrawlCustomConnector

▶ Remove-SPEnterpriseSearchCrawlDatabase

▶ Remove-SPEnterpriseSearchCrawlExtension

▶ Remove-SPEnterpriseSearchCrawlMapping

▶ Remove-SPEnterpriseSearchCrawlRule

▶ Remove-SPEnterpriseSearchCrawlLogReadPermission

▶ Remove-SPEnterpriseSearchCrawlLogReadPermission

Only a handful of cmdlets can be used to config crawl settings:

▶ Set-SPEnterpriseSearchCrawlContentSource

▶ Set-SPEnterpriseSearchCrawlDatabase

▶ Set-SPEnterpriseSearchCrawlRule

▶ Set-SPEnterpriseSearchCrawlLogReadPermission

Metadata

The full list of search metadata cmdlets follows:

▶ Get-SPEnterpriseSearchMetadataCategory

▶ Get-SPEnterpriseSearchMetadataCrawledProperty

▶ Get-SPEnterpriseSearchMetadataManagedProperty

▶ Get-SPEnterpriseSearchMetadataMapping

▶ Get-SPEnterpriseSearchPropertyRuleCollection

▶ Get-SPEnterpriseSearchPropertyRule

▶ New-SPEnterpriseSearchMetadataCategory

▶ New-SPEnterpriseSearchMetadataCrawledProperty

▶ New-SPEnterpriseSearchMetadataManagedProperty

▶ New-SPEnterpriseSearchMetadataMapping

▶ Remove-SPEnterpriseSearchMetadataCategory

▶ Remove-SPEnterpriseSearchMetadataManagedProperty

- Remove-SPEnterpriseSearchMetadataMapping
- Set-SPEnterpriseSearchMetadataCategory
- Set-SPEnterpriseSearchMetadataCrawledProperty
- Set-SPEnterpriseSearchMetadataManagedProperty
- Set-SPEnterpriseSearchMetadataMapping

Miscellaneous

Several cmdlets can be used to tweak certain areas and settings of Enterprise Search but can't be classified into a specific area. These cmdlets are as follows:

- Get-SPEnterpriseSearchLanguageResourcePhrase
- Get-SPEnterpriseSearchSiteHitRule
- Get-SPEnterpriseSearchLinksDatabase
- Get-SPEnterpriseSearchFileFormat
- Get-SPEnterpriseSearchComponent
- Get-SPEnterpriseSearchServiceApplicationBackupStore
- Get-SPEnterpriseSearchVssDataPath
- Get-SPEnterpriseSearchContentEnrichmentConfiguration
- Get-SPEnterpriseSearchLinguisticComponentsStatus
- Get-SPEnterpriseSearchHostController
- Import-SPEnterpriseSearchCustomExtractionDictionary
- New-SPEnterpriseSearchLanguageResourcePhrase
- New-SPEnterpriseSearchSiteHitRule
- New-SPEnterpriseSearchLinksDatabase
- New-SPEnterpriseSearchFileFormat
- New-SPEnterpriseSearchAnalyticsProcessingComponent
- New-SPEnterpriseSearchContentEnrichmentConfiguration
- Remove-SPEnterpriseSearchContentEnrichmentConfiguration
- Remove-SPEnterpriseSearchLanguageResourcePhrase
- Remove-SPEnterpriseSearchSiteHitRule
- Remove-SPEnterpriseSearchTenantSchema
- Remove-SPEnterpriseSearchTenantConfiguration
- Remove-SPEnterpriseSearchLinksDatabase
- Remove-SPEnterpriseSearchFileFormat

- ▶ Repartition-SPEnterpriseSearchLinksDatabases
- ▶ Set-SPEnterpriseSearchPrimaryHostController
- ▶ Set-SPEnterpriseSearchLinguisticComponentsStatus
- ▶ Set-SPEnterpriseSearchContentEnrichmentConfiguration
- ▶ Set-SPEnterpriseSearchLinksDatabase

Querying

To manage, tweak, and configure the querying in your SharePoint farm, the following cmdlets are available:

- ▶ Get-SPEnterpriseSearchQueryAndSiteSettingsService
- ▶ Get-SPEnterpriseSearchQueryAndSiteSettingsServiceInstance
- ▶ Get-SPEnterpriseSearchQueryAndSiteSettingsServiceProxy
- ▶ Get-SPEnterpriseSearchQueryAuthority
- ▶ Get-SPEnterpriseSearchQueryDemoted
- ▶ Get-SPEnterpriseSearchQueryKeyword
- ▶ Get-SPEnterpriseSearchQueryScope
- ▶ Get-SPEnterpriseSearchQueryScopeRule
- ▶ Get-SPEnterpriseSearchQuerySuggestionCandidates
- ▶ Get-SPEnterpriseSearchRankingModel
- ▶ Get-SPEnterpriseSearchSecurityTrimmer
- ▶ Get-SPEnterpriseSearchResultItemType
- ▶ Get-SPEnterpriseSearchQuerySpellingCorrection
- ▶ Import-SPEnterpriseSearchPopularQueries
- ▶ Import-SPEnterpriseSearchThesaurus
- ▶ New-SPEnterpriseSearchQueryAuthority
- ▶ New-SPEnterpriseSearchQueryDemoted
- ▶ New-SPEnterpriseSearchQueryKeyword
- ▶ New-SPEnterpriseSearchQueryScope
- ▶ New-SPEnterpriseSearchQueryScopeRule
- ▶ New-SPEnterpriseSearchRankingModel
- ▶ New-SPEnterpriseSearchSecurityTrimmer
- ▶ New-SPEnterpriseSearchResultItemType
- ▶ Remove-SPEnterpriseSearchQueryAuthority

▶ Remove-SPEnterpriseSearchQueryDemoted

▶ Remove-SPEnterpriseSearchQueryKeyword

▶ Remove-SPEnterpriseSearchQueryScope

▶ Remove-SPEnterpriseSearchQueryScopeRule

▶ Remove-SPEnterpriseSearchRankingModel

▶ Remove-SPEnterpriseSearchSecurityTrimmer

▶ Remove-SPEnterpriseSearchResultItemType

▶ Set-SPEnterpriseSearchQueryAuthority

▶ Set-SPEnterpriseSearchQueryKeyword

▶ Set-SPEnterpriseSearchQueryScope

▶ Set-SPEnterpriseSearchQueryScopeRule

▶ Set-SPEnterpriseSearchRankingModel

▶ Set-SPEnterpriseSearchResultItemType

▶ Set-SPEnterpriseSearchQuerySpellingCorrection

▶ Start-SPEnterpriseSearchQueryAndSiteSettingsServiceInstance

▶ Stop-SPEnterpriseSearchQueryAndSiteSettingsServiceInstance

Service Application

The search service application also comes loaded with configuration cmdlets listed here:

▶ Backup-SPEnterpriseSearchServiceApplicationIndex

▶ Get-SPEnterpriseSearchOwner

▶ Get-SPEnterpriseSearchService

▶ Get-SPEnterpriseSearchServiceApplication

▶ Get-SPEnterpriseSearchServiceApplicationProxy

▶ Get-SPEnterpriseSearchServiceInstance

▶ New-SPEnterpriseSearchServiceApplication

▶ New-SPEnterpriseSearchServiceApplicationProxy

▶ Remove-SPEnterpriseSearchServiceApplication

▶ Remove-SPEnterpriseSearchServiceApplicationProxy

▶ Restore-SPEnterpriseSearchServiceApplication

▶ Resume-SPEnterpriseSearchServiceApplication

▶ Restore-SPEnterpriseSearchServiceApplicationIndex

- Remove-SPEnterpriseSearchServiceApplicationSiteSettings
- Set-SPEnterpriseSearchService
- Set-SPEnterpriseSearchServiceApplication
- Set-SPEnterpriseSearchServiceApplicationProxy
- Start-SPEnterpriseSearchServiceInstance
- Stop-SPEnterpriseSearchServiceInstance
- Suspend-SPEnterpriseSearchServiceApplication
- Suspend-SPEnterpriseSearchServiceApplication
- Upgrade-SPEnterpriseSearchServiceApplication
- Upgrade-SPEnterpriseSearchServiceApplicationSiteSettings

Topology

In SharePoint 2013, you can now generate and configure the search topology on your farm using these cmdlets:

- Export-SPEnterpriseSearchTopology
- Get-SPEnterpriseSearchTopology
- Import-SPEnterpriseSearchTopology
- New-SPEnterpriseSearchTopology
- New-SPEnterpriseSearchQueryProcessingComponent
- New-SPEnterpriseSearchIndexComponent
- New-SPEnterpriseSearchContentProcessingComponent
- Remove-SPEnterpriseSearchTopology
- Remove-SPEnterpriseSearchComponent
- Set-SPEnterpriseSearchTopology

APPENDIX D

App Management Service Reference

SharePoint 2013 introduces an "app" paradigm for coded SharePoint solutions, along with an online store (or configurable on-premises marketplace). Several PowerShell cmdlets can be used when managing apps in SharePoint.

App Settings and Configuration

Use the cmdlets listed in this section to get or set app configuration settings:

- ▶ Get-SPAppAcquisitionSettings
- ▶ Get-SPAppAutoProvisionConnection
- ▶ Get-SPAppDomain
- ▶ Get-SPAppHostingQuotas
- ▶ Get-SPAppInstance
- ▶ Get-SPAppScaleProfile
- ▶ Get-SPAppDisableSettings
- ▶ Get-SPAppStateUpdateInterval
- ▶ Get-SPAppStateSyncLastRunTime
- ▶ Get-SPInternalAppStateSyncLastRunTime
- ▶ Get-SPInternalAppStateUpdateInterval
- ▶ Set-SPAppAcquisitionSettings
- ▶ Set-SPAppAutoProvisionConnection
- ▶ Set-SPAppDomain
- ▶ Set-SPAppHostingQuotas
- ▶ Set-SPAppManagementDeploymentId
- ▶ Set-SPAppMarketplaceSettings
- ▶ Set-SPAppScaleProfile

▸ `Set-SPAppStateDisableListSync`

▸ `Set-SPAppStateUpdateInterval`

▸ `Set-SPInternalAppStateUpdateInterval`

Denied Endpoint Management

The app structure in SharePoint 2013 enables you to configure denied endpoints. Use these PowerShell cmdlets to execute denied endpoint functions:

▸ `Add-SPAppDeniedEndpoint`

▸ `Clear-SPAppDeniedEndpoints`

▸ `Get-SPAppDeniedEndpoints`

▸ `Remove-SPAppDeniedEndpoint`

Installation and Provisioning of Apps

Use the following cmdlets to manage the installation of apps and app packages:

▸ `Disable-SPAppAutoProvision`

▸ `Enable-SPAppAutoProvision`

▸ `Export-SPAppPackage`

▸ `Import-SPAppPackage`

▸ `Install-SPApp`

▸ `Restart-SPAppInstanceJobs`

▸ `Uninstall-SPAppInstance`

▸ `Update-SPAppCatalogSettings`

▸ `Update-SPAppInstance`

Marketplace Management

Use the following cmdlets to manage the marketplace and Office Store settings:

▸ `Get-SPAppMarketplaceSettings`

▸ `Get-SPMarketplaceConnectionSettings`

▸ `Get-SPAppSiteSubscriptionName`

▸ `Get-SPOfficeStoreAppsDefaultActivation`

- `New-SPMarketplaceWebServiceApplicationProxy`
- `Set-SPMarketplaceConnectionSettings`
- `Set-SPAppSiteSubscriptionName`
- `Set-SPOfficeStoreAppsDefaultActivation`

Service Application

As far as the App Service application is concerned, you can only use SharePoint PowerShell to create a new service application or new service application proxy using their respective cmdlets:

- `New-SPAppManagementServiceApplication`
- `New-SPAppManagementServiceApplicationProxy`

Index

Symbols

/ (forward slashes), 34
-?, nouns, 10

A

Access Services, 218

application log size, configuring, 218
cache timeout, configuring, 218-219
configuring
maximum number of records in tables, 221
maximum number of rows in queries, 220-221
maximum number of sources in queries, 222
maximum Order By clauses, 220
modifying
databases, 226
maximum calculated columns in queries, 219-220
maximum columns in queries, 219
nonremotable queries, allow/restrict, 223
outer joins, 222-223
template sizes, limiting, 225-226
throttling, 224
session memory utilization, 224-225
user sessions, configuring, 225
actions, disabling in WOPI, 247
activating
features, 95
forms, site collection, 117
sandboxed solutions, 91-92
ActiveProcesses parameter, 234
ActiveSessionTimeout, 114
AddEnabledFileExtensions, 188
Add-SPSolution, 86

X

Y-Z

STEVEN MANN

PowerShell for SharePoint 2013 HOW-TO

SAMS

FREE
Online Edition

Safari Books Online

Your purchase of *PowerShell for SharePoint 2013 How-To* includes access to a free online edition for 45 days through the **Safari Books Online** subscription service. Nearly every Addison-Wesley Professional book is available online through **Safari Books Online**, along with thousands of books and videos from publishers such as Cisco Press, Exam Cram, IBM Press, O'Reilly Media, Prentice Hall, Que, and Sams.

Safari Books Online is a digital library providing searchable, on-demand access to thousands of technology, digital media, and professional development books and videos from leading publishers. With one monthly or yearly subscription price, you get unlimited access to learning tools and information on topics including mobile app and software development, tips and tricks on using your favorite gadgets, networking, project management, graphic design, and much more.

Activate your FREE Online Edition at
informit.com/safarifree

STEP 1: Enter the coupon code: CXIXEBI.

STEP 2: New Safari users, complete the brief registration form.
Safari subscribers, just log in.

If you have difficulty registering on Safari or accessing the online edition,
please e-mail customer-service@safaribooksonline.com

IT SERVICES
COVENTRY UNIVERSITY

 Addison Wesley
 AdobePress ALPHA
Cisco Press
 FT Press
 IBM Press
 Microsoft Press
 New Riders
 O'REILLY

 Peachpit Press
 PRENTICE HALL
 que
 Redbooks
 SAMS
 SAS Publishing
 vmware PRESS
 WILEY
 wrox

PowerShell™ for SharePoint® 2013
HOW-TO

Need fast, reliable, easy-to-implement solutions for automating SharePoint 2013 administration with PowerShell? This guide delivers exactly what you're looking for: step-by-step help and guidance with the tasks you'll perform most often. You'll find tested PowerShell scripts and techniques for managing installations, servers, farms, IIS, users, services, sites, data, solutions, enterprise services, search, PerformancePoint business intelligence, and more. This edition adds time-saving techniques for managing user licensing and new SharePoint 2013 service applications, covers new cmdlets, and contains two new reference appendices. This focused resource for scripting SharePoint with PowerShell provides all the answers you need—*now*!

Steven Mann, Enterprise Applications Engineer for Morgan Lewis, has nearly 20 years of professional experience. As Principal Architect for RDA Corporation, he focused on collaboration, search, and business intelligence solutions using Microsoft technologies for more than eight years. His SharePoint books include *InfoPath with SharePoint 2010 How-To*, *Microsoft SharePoint 2010 Business Intelligence Unleashed*, *SharePoint 2010 Field Guide*, and *SharePoint 2010 Managed Metadata Unleashed*. Mann founded Philly SNUG: Center City Philadelphia User's Group for SharePoint and .NET Professionals.

On the Web:
Register your book to download examples and source code presented in this book from **www.informit.com/title/9780672336911.**

Category: Microsoft SharePoint
User Level: Intermediate

ISBN-13: 978-0-672-33691-1
ISBN-10: 0-672-33691-X

$34.99 US / $36.99 CAN

Fast, Accurate, and Easy to Us

► Run PowerShell scripts from the SharePoint 2013 Management Shell console

► Perform unattended SharePoint installations

► Configure new farms, add servers, and manage sites

► Create new site collections and sub-sites

► Review and set Farm Configura Values and SharePoint Designer Settings

► Display, get, create, remove, configure, and extend web applications

► Create, manage, remove, back and restore SharePoint databas

► Work with SharePoint solutions and features

► Automatically publish and manage content

► Establish and change external data connections via Business Data Connectivity Service

► Control the new versions of Exc Access, Visio, and Word Servic

► Script Office Web Apps to deliv more robust web/mobile solutic

► Manage PerformancePoint business intelligence via cmdlet

► Administer Enterprise Search, InfoPath Form Services, profiles metadata, and Secure Store

► Streamline Work Management Services to help users track tasks more efficiently

SAMS
informit.com/sams

ALWAYS LEARNING

PEARSON